The Muny
St. Louis' Outdoor Theater

The Muny
St. Louis' Outdoor Theater

by Mary Kimbrough

The Bethany Press
St. Louis, Missouri

Cover and text design by Roger Siebe

Photos courtesy St. Louis Municipal Opera

Library of Congress Cataloguing in Publication Data

Kimbrough, Mary.
  The Muny: St. Louis' outdoor theater.
    1. St. Louis. Municipal Opera. I. Title.
ML1711.8.S15M85   782.8'1'06277866   78-6847
ISBN 0-8272-2315-3
ISBN 0-8272-2314-5 pbk.

Distributed in Canada by the G. R. Welch Company, Ltd., Toronto, Ontario,
Canada
Printed in the United States of America

Contents

Prologue

For nearly sixty years now they've called it the "Muny," a plain little word which means to St. Louisans a wondrous world of fantasy.

It's a chameleon-like creation that is transformed by the alchemy of art from a lavish, legendary kingdom into the loneliness of desert sands, from raucous street to the sun-drenched deck of a showboat on the levee. Before your very eyes, waterfalls plummet from hidden sources somewhere in the wings, mountains rise in majesty from a wooden floor, and gardens bloom in concrete.

It's a time machine set to music, transporting all who watch into another age; breaking, in the whisper of a moment, the flimsy barriers of the years and of the miles.

The city has crawled westward to encircle it; yet, when the sun goes down and the lights go up, the Muny separates itself from the city's cares and chaos. For this is a special place of pretending, an island of imagery, where tales are spun and songs are sung and, for a brief hour, illusion is substance and the dream is truth.

From its first sixty years could emerge a plot as dramatic as any played upon its stage. Its story is as bittersweet as a song of lost love, as suspenseful as the perils of Pauline, as enduring as laughter.

This, then, is the Muny as it enters its sixtieth year: an oak grown tall from an acorn dream, corporate enterprise in woodland quiet, a lusty legend that couldn't die. It's the warm informality of the straw hat circuit and the artistry of the Met. It's Broadway on the Mississippi, the Great White Way carved out of a midwestern hillside, show business beneath the stars. It's P. T. Barnum and Flo Ziegfeld and Cecil B. De Mille. The Palace and the Hippodrome, the Big Top and Carnegie Hall.

But, most of all, it's a make-believe world brushed by midsummer madness. A magical world wrapped in a song.

THE world may spin in the cold age of space, and the voice of the computer may be heard in the land. But the softness of another summer has brought back the Muny and, like flashbacks on a screen, memories of the passing years.

". . . an enduring monument of its coming; a souvenir which, in many coming nights of light and beauty, will serve us for remembrance." (*St. Louis Globe-Democrat,* June 8, 1917, commenting on the Pageant Drama Association's performance of *Aida,* a forerunner of the Muny.)

An aerial shot shows the tiers of audience and the covered walk-
ways along the sides of the Muny theater.

Chapter 1

Babes in Toyland

THE tall trees on the Forest Park hillside were still dripping from the afternoon's summer storm and the ground beneath them was soggy to the step.

But despite the clouds that lingered to blur the skies, nearly 4,000 St. Louisans with their raincoats and umbrellas, some in formal dress, had climbed the concrete tiers to their places in the big, spoon-shaped amphitheater, waiting with genial impatience for that invisible curtain to rise.

The year was 1919. The guns of war to end all wars were once again silent and the boys had come home to be cheered to the skies as they paraded through downtown St. Louis. In the air was a feeling of hope, a sense of well-being, a mingling of excitement and joy. It was a good time to start something new.

And so on that Monday, June 16, at exactly 8:25 P.M., the trumpeted melody of the National Anthem rang through Forest Park. The sudden scuffle of folding wooden chairs on concrete added a discordant note to the music as the audience rose.

They would never forget this night, these hardy 4,000, for they were watching the dawn of a bold experiment by a handful of audacious men. Never mind that these men were not theater magnates or actors or singers or producers. They were officeholders and advertising men and businessmen and merchants who had walked into the strange and eye-popping world of show business. They were eager amateurs in the world of make-up and make-believe, footlights and fantasy —St. Louis' own *Babes in Toyland.*

But now it was 8:30. The audience had hardly settled back before the baton was raised again, the chatter was muffled, and the Reginald De Koven overture soared into the air.

Robin Hood had begun.

And with its first words and music, spoken and sung in the softness of a summer night, was born the St. Louis Municipal Opera.

The cynics said it was a crazy scheme that couldn't last. They called it a midsummer night's dream gone awry, a legend stillborn, a gaudy gamble that would end before it could get started.

They were almost right.

Of course, it was a crazy scheme, one no American city had ever tried before. And, within a week, the weatherman would try to wash it down the River Des Peres as surely as Ensign Nellie Forbush, in *South Pacific,* would someday try to wash that man right out of her hair at this very spot.

But the scoffers and the cynics were wrong about one thing. Dead wrong. They couldn't believe the little opera could survive one season, let alone outlive all of them. They couldn't imagine that it would become a world-renowned theatrical landmark, attract the most luminous show business names to its stage and generations of enchanted watchers to this same hillside.

They didn't know this was the beginning of a new American theatrical tradition, the outdoor summer musical. Many cities would follow St. Louis' lead. None would ever match the Muny.

Even those who believed in it, this midsummer night in 1919, might not have dared to look down the future and predict how much the infant Muny would grow by the dawn of its sixtieth season.

It was miracle enough that they had brought it this far.

True, the dreams and hard work and nerve and muscle of thousands of other St. Louisans in earlier years had converged into this special moment like a genealogical chart.

The Municipal Opera's ancestral roots lie deep in the green turf of Forest Park, and its bloodlines flow back to a wondrous World's Fair.

It is descended from a magnificent Pageant and Masque on Art Hill; a lovely Shakespearean play in a tranquil glen which would later become the Muny's birthplace and permanent home; a grand opera presented for the world's advertising men and women, and a four-day Pageant of Independence, *Fighting for Freedom.*

Forest Park was a natural showplace for all of these. The Louisiana Purchase Exposition of 1904, a splendid spectacle the likes of which the world had never seen, proved that. It would be another ten years, however, before the 1,400-acre parkland at the city's edge would become the site of a second show business spectacular.

In 1914, to mark the 150th birthday of St. Louis, a group of citizens, headed by John Gundlach, Charlotte Rumbold, director of the first recreation department, and Dwight Davis, park commissioner, organized the St. Louis Pageant Drama Association.

That May, they put on an extravaganza which the *St. Louis Globe-Democrat,* in editorial ebullience, called "the greatest show in history."

The Pageant and Masque of St. Louis.

The pageant was written and directed by the illustrious Thomas Wood Stevens, followed with the masque by the equally-renowned Percy MacKay. Joseph Lindon Smith was the producer and Frederick Converse wrote the score. Two St. Louisans, Noel Poepping and Ernest R. Kroeger, composed incidental music.

It featured a cast of more than 7000, all eager volunteers from St. Louis. As other thousands watched from their places on Art Hill, a galaxy of performers recreated the past on a 520 × 200-foot stage built over the lagoon.

In 1918 the builders are just beginning to convert the hillside of the Muny to an organized and permanent seating arrangement.

There were covered wagons and stagecoaches, Indians and mound builders and horses and oxen and baskets and boats. There were Mayan temples and crumbling ruins and Civil War troops and Marquette and Pierre Laclede, Joliet and Lafayette, and electric lights flashing out the constellation of Missouri's Great Bear. All in all, it was quite a show.

From all across America they came, arriving by boat and train and, if they lived close enough, by streetcar or on foot. Nearly a half-million watched, with an estimated 175,000 at one performance alone.

They all agreed it should be an annual event. But, unlike the still-to-be-born Muny, the Pageant and Masque was destined to have only one shot at glory. It ended after a three-night run, never to return.

Even so, the dream of a permanent outdoor theater had been planted in the civic heart and nourished by the Pageant's heady success. Two years later, in 1916, the Pageant

This is an audience on the hillside at the earliest photographed show which was the forerunner of the modern Muny Opera.

Drama Association invited the distinguished Shakespearean actress, Margaret Anglin, to star in *As You Like It* to memorialize the 300th anniversary of the dramatist's death.

But leaders of the Association soon realized that Art Hill, so spectacular and natural a setting for the massive Masque, was inappropriate for the Shakespearean production. A more suitable site must be found.

Like early-day explorers searching for treasure, they tracked through the woodland of Forest Park. On the banks of the River Des Peres, they paused. A little hill rose gently from a level, grassy, natural stage. Two magnificent oak trees stood at either side like stately sentinels, and as the St. Louisans stood there they could imagine the trees' leafy branches forming a proscenium arch of green.

This, surely, was it. Tucked away in the middle of a city, Shakespeare's serene Forest of Arden.

They didn't know that someday this would be the Muny.

When she saw the site, Margaret Anglin was enchanted. Then the indefatigable Nelson Cunliff, the city's superintendent of construction who later would be a founding father of the Opera, went to work to transform the hillside into a theater. He transplanted shrubs and trees, spanned the Des Peres with a rustic bridge, set up spotlights, built cinder paths and wooden tiers on the slope. A retaining wall was constructed to level the stage.

On Monday, June 5, all was ready for that evening's opening performance.

It rained.

On Tuesday, June 6, all was ready for the postponed opening performance.

It rained.

On Wednesday, June 7, it rained again. This time, though, the skies suddenly cleared and in the soggy theater, before a damp, yet enchanted crowd, the show went on. It was a brilliant success even as had been the Pageant and Masque before it.

Appearing with Miss Anglin were the greats of the day and the lesser-known who would find greatness with the years: Robert Mantell, Frederick Lewis, Henry Hull, Genevieve Hamper, Louis Calhern, and John Alexander. Sydney Greenstreet, later to become a sinister fat man in Hollywood, was Touchstone, the clown, and a young actor named Alfred Lunt played two minor roles.

When it was over, Mantell, one of the most prestigious Shakespearean actors in the history of the American theater, said the Forest Park stage "would gain for St. Louis a reputation for having a perfect open-air theater and enough enthusiasm to utilize it."

Miss Anglin agreed. She prophesied that the little edifice open to the midwestern stars and carved out of a tree-shaded parkland many miles from Broadway, would become "one of the most noted outdoor theaters in the world."

Her prediction and that of Mantell echoed the prophecy of Percy MacKay who, two years earlier, had declared:

"This is only the beginning. The movement will not die in the city which first gave birth to it through the cooperation of its citizens."

They were three wise prophets, indeed.

In the pleasant aftermath of the Shakespearean observance, with the Pageant and Masque still fresh in civic memory, St. Louis began to wonder what to do with its new open-air theater which owned at least a semblance of permanence.

It was the Advertising Club of St. Louis which offered a solution and, in the process, laid the foundation for the Municipal Opera.

The Associated Advertising Clubs of the World would be meeting here in the summer of 1917. The Club asked the city: Why not concrete the amphitheater to make it really permanent, improve the stage and facilities, and put on an evening of grand opera for visiting dignitaries and delegates?

Mayor Henry W. Kiel quickly recognized the potential benefit to his city and endorsed the idea. Nelson Cunliff, now park commissioner, was enthusiastic. The Board of Aldermen and the Board of Public Service approved and granted a building permit.

To help finance the project, the Advertising Club agreed to buy $5,000 in tickets, even though, at the moment, the tickets were for an unselected show by an unnamed cast in a theater which hadn't been built.

But the next morning, work was begun. And forty-two days later, the wooden tiers had been replaced by concrete and St. Louis had a permanent outdoor theater.

Meanwhile, Verdi's *Aida* had been selected as the attraction at the suggestion of Guy Golterman of the St. Louis Grand Opera Committee, who would produce it. Now, working with as much speed as the construction crews, he assembled a brilliant cast headed by Frances Peralta and Manual Salazar.

The artists arrived in St. Louis May 27 to start rehearsals, and on June 5, 1917, the stately operatic arias were sung on the same tree-shaded spot where Shakespeare's lovely poetry had been spoken just a year earlier.

The scintillating performance echoed across the world. From Paris, the illustrious diva, Mary Garden, cabled: "Have just heard of latest achievement in St. Louis which means much to lyric drama. Congratulations and best wishes."

It was an enchanted evening in St. Louis. It also was a wet one.

PROGRAM
AS YOU LIKE IT

WITH A
COMMUNITY EPILOGUE

PRESENTED BY
THE ST. LOUIS PAGEANT DRAMA ASSOCIATION

IN HONOR OF WILLIAM SHAKESPEARE
IN THE 300TH YEAR AFTER HIS DEATH

AT THE

MUNICIPAL OPEN-AIR THEATRE
FOREST PARK, SAINT LOUIS

EIGHT PERFORMANCES
BEGINNING MONDAY, JUNE FIFTH
EVENINGS AT SEVEN FORTY-FIVE O'CLOCK

MATINEE SATURDAY, JUNE TENTH
AT THREE P. M.

A program honoring Shakespeare in 1916 set the scene for what was to become the St. Louis Muny Opera.

Robin Hood in 1927 was a lavish, spectacular show.

The same stormy fate which descended on Shakespeare, and later would return to haunt the newborn Muny, almost drowned the debut of *Aida*.

In his book, *St. Louis' Fabulous Municipal Theatre,* published in 1969, Charles V. Clifford recreates the scene.

"Because of threatening weather, a number of persons were late arriving and as conditions grew worse some of the crowd began leaving, causing much confusion.

"The impending storm broke about 10 o'clock, shortly after Radames, in a chariot drawn by two horses, had made his triumphal entry in the imposing second act with several hundred persons on the stage. The principals and many of the chorus members continued singing in the rain until the end of the act while the audience raised their umbrellas. It was impossible to present the last half of the program because of the downpour."

Happily, the skies cleared, and the opera was presented the next three scheduled nights with an extra performance as a make-up at the end of the run.

Now the theater in the park was, indeed, a permanent civic attraction, and it became a favorite platform for other grand opera, for fashion shows and festivals, games and concerts. None was grander or, perhaps, more significant for the future of the Muny than the patriotic pageant, *Fighting for Freedom,* created by Thomas Wood Stevens with a cast of nearly 1,000, and presented over the July 4th holiday in 1918.

The pageant, with proceeds to go to a community war fund, had been developed by the city, and on May 2 of that year, the Municipal Theatre Association had been formed, with Mayor Kiel as president, to put on the spectacular show.

Four months later, with the return of peace, again the question arose: what was the future of the open air theater in the park, a theater not very grand, to be sure, but a natural edifice with the glory of the skies and the stars as its roof and a gentle slope as its auditorium?

Let one who was there take up the story.

Ralf Toensfeldt, a consulting engineer who at his death in 1971 was the last surviving founder of the Muny, wrote in *The Pepper Box,* official organ of the Rotary Club of St. Louis:

"At the conclusion of the war, a group of men, Art Siegel, Max Koenigsberg, Nelson Cunliff, G. A. Buder, and Walter

Donaldson, met in Mayor Kiel's office to consider the future of a magnificent open-air theater. . . . It, of course, was not a complete theater. It had a crude wood stage, it had no lighting system, it had no shelters for the audience in case of rain, nor did it have any dressing rooms. . . ."

But it was St. Louis' own, and now the five men asked themselves how it could best be used. More Shakespeare, as some in the cultural community argued? Grand opera? A repertory theater?

"Henry Kiel and his intimates," continued Toensfeldt, "remembered Schnaiders Gardens, they remembered Uhrig's Cave, they remembered Suburban Gardens and Delmar Gardens, all of them producing light opera and musical events. . . . They remembered the Damrosch Opera Company and Sousa and Gilmore's Band and the two 20-week seasons of the Castle Square Opera Company at the old Exposition Hall at Thirteenth and Olive."

They looked back and remembered and, in the musical heritage of St. Louis, they found their answer. They would offer light opera to the public.

The decision of those men that day in 1919 was destined to change the cultural course of their city and launch a glittering legend.

The die was cast. The Muny had come into being. The sound of music was in Forest Park to stay.

At the beginning, it would be a simple melody, for there were far more dreams than dollars. And, through the years, sour notes would sometimes mar the harmony.

But now, in the spring of 1919, there was too much work to be done to worry about the future.

On March 6, plans were set in motion to present six operas, the season to begin June 16. That was just a little over four months away.

First, the money. In a matter of days, $27,500 was raised as a guarantors' fund to be used only in dire need. That would begin a sturdy tradition of civic and business involvement through which, each year, firms and individuals would become opera guarantors. Only twice in the next sixty years would the guaranty fund be used. Each time, it would be paid back to the penny.

In April, St. Louisans were invited to vote on the repertory and, from their ballots, the first season was organized. *Robin Hood* would start it off.

A committee was dispatched to New York to engage stars who would remain for the entire season as a stock company. Others were recruited from acting troupes in St. Louis. Signed for the season were Caroline Andrews, Stella de Mette, Mildred Rogers, Frank Moulan, Blanche Duffield, Craig Campbell, Carl Gantvoort, Charles E. Galagher, William Danforth. The first musical director was John McGhie and the first stage director, Charles T. H. Jones.

St. Louis musicians were auditioned for a huge chorus, to be augmented by some forty professionals from the east, and rehearsals began at the Jefferson Memorial and at the Rialto Theatre—later Loew's Mid-City on Grand Avenue.

Ticket prices were set, twenty-five cents to one dollar, and 1,620 of the 9,000 seats were set aside as free, a tradition which was to continue over the years.

Meanwhile, the theater was undergoing a face-lift and minor surgery. Although its appearance and facilities were a tribute to civic ingenuity, with its borrowed and make-do equipment, it still was a pale and almost primitive forerunner of the sophisticated theatrical world it was destined to become.

"Scenery," wrote Ralf Toensfeldt, "was designed by a local architect and painted by local artists. It consisted of 'flats,' generally used in the theater at that time, held up by stage braces screwed to the floor.

"Lighting equipment consisted of two tall telephone poles borrowed from Bell Telephone . . . dimmers consisted of water barrels filled with salt water, the electrical switchboard was left over from the Pageant and Masque. . . . Dressing rooms for principals were only rough sheds built on stilts across the river from the stage. . . . Chorus dressing rooms were tents. . . ."

On June 10, 1919, the Municipal Theatre Association gained official status with a pro forma decree of incorporation and six days later, on Monday, June 16, the invisible curtain rose on *Robin Hood*.

It was not altogether an artistic success although a local critic was kindly-disposed toward the new baby in town.

22

St. Louis Mayor Henry Kiel appeared as King Richard in the 1918
version of *Robin Hood.*

"Last night's essay was to all intents and purposes a tryout for all concerned," he wrote, "to which the difficulties of a dampened stage and a general air of moisture and sogginess after Monday afternoon's downpour must be added and, in the same sense of fairness, due allowance must be made. . . .

"Mayor Kiel congratulated the company on the furtherance of an enterprise which he felt would 'redound greatly to the fame of the city as an art center of first importance . . .'"

The doughty Mayor, within the week, was to wonder if he had spoken too soon.

Chapter 2

The Unsinkable Molly Brown

EARLY on the morning of Monday, June 23, 1919, just a week after Mayor Kiel had uttered his hopeful words, his dream almost went down the drain and the Muny down the Mississippi.

In the rain-swept first week of the Muny's life, *Robin Hood* had merely been drenched—but at the beginning of the second week, *The Bohemian Girl* just about drowned as the weatherman, like a misanthrope with a tin ear, flexed his muscles for a knockout blow.

On that infamous Monday, a catastrophic cloudburst struck the city and, tragically, two young boys were swept to their deaths in the swirling waters of the River Des Peres which ran right by the Opera in Forest Park.

By noon, the opening performance of *The Bohemian Girl* had been postponed until Tuesday night. There was nothing else they could do. The water was four feet deep. The stage itself was about the only thing left standing.

"The River Des Peres," wrote Ralf Toensfeldt in *The Pepper Box,* "left its banks, the two bridges (backstage at the

Opera) were washed out, the scenery went downstream, bass fiddles followed.

"But the faithful were not to be daunted. The scenery and instruments were found as far away as Carondelet. They were brought to the theater, dried out and refurbished. The bridges were rebuilt and the show was ready the next night and went on as though nothing had happened."

Something, however, did happen. Six minutes more and they would have made it.

A disgusted newspaper critic reported it in poetic detail in the next day's *St. Louis Globe-Democrat*.

"It might be well to know that there were other actors, not on the stage but far above it. Jupiter Tonaris with his rumbling thunder sheet and well assorted parcels of lightning bolts. Jupiter Pluvius, ready with tons of condensing vapors. Zephyr, Aconius and other classic windmakers, far aloft, right behind Venus who could not show the big audience her fairest face because the celestial stage was set for the customary downpour.

"Lowering clouds began to enshroud the goddess soon after Conductor McGhie had intoned 'The Star Spangled Banner'. . . .

"At 10:40, it came, the dreaded rain. At the moment when the last ensemble selection of 'The Bo Girl' was being sung, that tuneful and appropriate chorus, 'Come away, Come away,' the storm broke and the audience needed no second cue. They likewise broke. . . ."

It was a soggy prelude of troubles yet to come.

Throughout the season, the weather reports would echo through the press like a gloomy refrain.

". . . The stage was wet enough to stain the pretty fleshings of the shapely chorus and the little bare-limbed dancers blackened the soles of their tingling feet . . ."

". . . Heavy regal costumes caused their wearers much physical discomfort in the thick, muggy atmosphere of the park. The big kettledrums couldn't be employed and the orchestra struggled valiantly against adverse weather conditions and the scenery showed water marks. . . ."

The big local chorus, it was reported, dwindled to sixty because parents of some teenagers felt that the damp stage was dangerous.

With gradually clearing skies by late June, the crowds picked up, but not enough. To bolster attendance, the Association decided to substitute two lighter operas, *The Wizard of the Nile* and *The Chimes of Normandy* for *Fra Diavolo* and *Carmen.* John Philip Sousa's sprightly *El Capitan* and the perennial favorite, *The Mikado,* by Gilbert and Sullivan, would complete the summer bill.

Still, the money was running out. In the first three weeks, it was announced, only $24,000 had been taken in and expenses amounted to $81,000.

The baby Muny appeared to be in as much trouble as a Broadway turkey and in as much danger of folding.

Officers of the Association had been turned down for a bank loan, but the bank president had agreed to co-sign their personal note. Now they had enough, at least, to meet the payroll. They also had a frightening deficit.

Mayor Kiel called an emergency meeting. Only five turned up. Someone suggested, as a grim joke, that the Mayor might have to go out himself and peddle tickets.

That's just what he did. He went up and down the business streets, urging, cajoling merchants to take blocks of seats. He organized a city-wide blitz. The newspapers got behind him. People began to buy. Clubs and committees organized Opera "nights."

And, at last, the invalid had passed the crisis. The deficit began to dwindle and the crowds began to grow.

There would be more headaches. There would be mistakes. It would be another two years, at least, before the Muny could be said to be out of the "experimental stage." But, at last, it was on its way.

Trouble, however, wasn't limited to the box office.

"The limitations of such an undertaking as that which the Municipal Opera under the musical direction of John McGhie is now forwarding toward accomplishment," a newspaperman wrote, "namely singing one opera while rehearsing for next week and forgetting what was learned in the week previous, were apparent in the 'El Capitan' premiere. . . .

"Lines were not memorizable to the fullest extent, stage directions were slighted and much of the necessary business of the action had to be slurred over."

Even so, by late July, the cynics who had predicted the Muny's early death had quieted down and the box office was singing a happier tune.

The stars, who had suffered with the city during the Muny's growing pains, volunteered to present a benefit concert the night after the season closed to help offset the deficit.

On the next-to-last night of the season, a record crowd of 8,200 attended *The Chimes of Normandy,* proving, as a reporter wrote, that the Opera's "fame seems to have permeated all of St. Louis."

Then, at last, on July 26, the Muny's first season came to an end. Joy, relief, hope and even a few tears must have mingled with the melody on that starlit night as Mildred Rogers, at Mayor Kiel's request, sang, "The End of a Perfect Day."

Then, as a reporter wrote, "Conductor John McGhie gave the signal for everyone to join in 'Auld Lang Syne' and the echoes of Forest Park in its midnight gloom were awakened with that heartfelt and sonorous atrophe. . . .

"The trumpets and the trombones rather emphasized the concluding stanza and made a joyful noise. . . ."

The "joyful noise" of "Auld Lang Syne" was to become, even as the Muny itself, a St. Louis legend, ringing down the invisible curtain on each successive season to come.

Mayor Kiel told the audience that night that the deficit had been cut down to $6,000.

"I believe the Municipal Opera," he said, "has established itself, and that it will be repeated every year."

At the end of the first show, his words had been those of the eternal optimist, whistling in the dark.

At the end of the season, his words were those of a prophet.

For the fledgling venture, a dream held together with chewing gum and baling wire, there would not always be fair skies or a song at the end of a perfect day. There would be more storms, even catastrophe.

But the Muny, like the indomitable Molly Brown, would not sink.

Chapter 3

Guys and Dolls

NO matter how cloudy the skies over Forest Park or how rain-swept the hillside, the "stars" always shine at the Muny.

They are stars in robes and rags, in prince's cloak and pauper's shawl. Stars in tights and tutus and tatters, in ballet slippers and boots. Stars clad in the opulence of the Orient, in the stark uniform of the street. Stars with fat scrapbooks and garish memories and would-be stars with gaudy dreams.

They didn't always get name-in-lights billing, even the greatest of them. In the Muny's earliest days, that accolade was lavished on the production itself, for all—backstage and front—shared the job of putting the show together and received, in turn, a portion of the publicity and the applause.

Not until the mid-50s, when television had mastered the fine art of manufacturing instant stardom, did artists' names begin to appear over show titles on the Muny programs.

In the 1930s and 1940s, featured players were imported for three or four or five roles a season, with local talent recruited for minor parts. Earlier, the cast, assembled here for the summer, was a stock company and the role of each member was pre-determined by talent and age and figure and specialty, whether it be prima donna, ingenue, comedian or—if ever needed in those days of fairyland repertoire—the heavy.

That didn't always work so well. One early player, cast in the role of an older woman, walked out in a huff.

Still, those pioneer players, as they struggled against the sometimes amazing odds through the Muny's early life, must have wondered, along with the cynics, if this could really last, if the peculiar magic they had wrought with their make-believe would ever become a part of St. Louis' heart and soul or just a pleasant footnote in a civic scrapbook.

They needn't have wasted the worry. They were destined to be theatrical trailblazers, the vanguard of a vast parade of star-struck guys and dolls who would follow them across the Muny stage in the many seasons yet to come.

It has been a lively procession. A thousand show business faces. A thousand show business hearts. There have been stars of first magnitude who shone with steady, brilliant luminance; minor stars of lesser light; talented choristers waiting in the wings.

There have been distinguished ballet companies, bands, and whole troupes simply lifted from Broadway and set down in St. Louis, stars with their galaxies of satellite performers. Hollywood's legends and Broadway's immortals.

The parade of players is a blend of triumph and temperament and, sometimes, tragedy. Of petulance and pique, of hits and flops and stage fright, of calamities and standing ovations.

For many, the Muny is another stop on an already glittering career. For others, it brings the first sweet taste of show business and becomes their own yellow brick road to glory. But all are bound together in that special world where happiness is the smell of grease paint and the sound of applause.

Leonard Ceeley, one of the Muny's most popular stars in the early 1930s, said it for everyone:

"We players are incurable romanticists. We get our very bread and butter from the land of make-believe. The fascination of the stage lies largely, I suspect, in the fact that each new play, each new role is an adventure."

30

A highly esteemed tenor in 1937 was Leonard Ceeley.

It certainly must have been an adventure for those earliest players when the Muny was beginning to grow from its first crude stage and seats on a concrete hillside into the world's largest outdoor theater and one of the best-known talent showcases between Broadway and Hollywood.

They dressed in makeshift quarters, clambered over rustic bridges which spanned the little River Des Peres and led to the backstage area. Unaccustomed to the grand dimensions of the 90 × 115-foot stage, they sometimes ran out of words or music before they could get where they were supposed to be.

Until the first sounding board was installed the second season, they had to depend on their own vocal power to reach the top rows. Even so, in that year's repeat of the 1919 inaugural, *Robin Hood,* they had to contend with a waterfall which, the reviewer said, "by its roaring and purlings over papier maché cliffs literally drowned the singers' sweet and kindly voices and jarred the thin orchestral harmonies."

But the Muny's early problems weren't all behind the footlights. Turbulence also was swirling behind the scenes.

Through apparently faulty casting, when the 1920 prima donna was assigned the star role of Maid Marian in *Robin Hood,* someone realized, too late, that her voice wasn't high enough, and she had to be asked to step aside for a substitute, Anne Bussart.

James Stevens, the resident baritone, left the company, it was reported, "to regain vocal health" in the Ozarks.

Delivering his replacement must have been a frantic scene worthy of the Keystone Kops. Frantically summoned from New York, Arthur Burckley was literally dragged off the train—which had arrived in St. Louis at 5:35 P.M., an hour late—was rehearsed on a wild drive to the theater and had one brief run-through with the cast before going on stage. He didn't muff a line or miss a cue.

There have been changes brought about by new stage technologies, new schools of thought, new breeds of performer and playwright and producer.

The Muny would gradually move from repertory company to star system. Big names would zoom in for a week, or just an evening, and zoom out again to the next booking. Friml and Kern and Romberg would begin to give way to Loesser and Loewe and Bob Fosse, *The Merry Widow* to Liza Minnelli and *The Student Prince* to Roy Clark and "The Grand Ole Muny Opry."

But some things just don't die. The face-to-face communication across the footlights, as intangible as air, as friendly as a Rotarian handshake, as instant as an electric spark. The excitement of opening night; the nostalgia when the last lights dim. The sound of applause cascading like a waterfall down the concrete tiers from highest free seats to front box.

A lot of famous ears have heard that sound. The Muny is the Palace of outdoor theaters and it's a rare star who misses it.

Some were already great when they got here. Pearl Bailey and Bob Hope and Ethel Merman and Carol Channing. Margot Fonteyn and Rudolph Nureyev, Cyril Ritchard, Dinah Shore, Carol Burnett and the Carpenters. The Hudson Brothers and the Andrews Sisters.

Some were on their way up. Irene Dunne was one, and Cary Grant (they called him Archie Leach then), Allan Jones, June Havoc. Virginia Mayo was a member of the chorus and so was Virginia Gibson. Gretchen Wienecke was "the big blonde at the left end of the chorus line." She came back, as Gretchen Wyler, to star.

Another star who has returned to Muny after achieving fame on both the Broadway stage and on network television is Mary Wickes. A native St. Louisan, she came back to the city where she got her start, appearing at Muny in no less than eleven productions.

For sixty years, the Muny has been a showcase for the stars. For the hopefuls, it has been a springboard to fame, a ticket on the big chance, a swipe at the brass ring. Some would fade into that performers' purgatory where applause is faint and the telephone doesn't ring.

Guy Robertson, one of the most popular stars of the early 1930s, went on to Hollywood, then to Broadway to star in *Of Mice and Men*. Queenie Smith co-starred with Lanny Ross in *Mississippi*.

When the Municipal Opera presented the world premiere of Jerome Kern's *Gentlemen Unafraid* in 1938, listed among "others" in the cast was a young comic named Richard Skelton. The reviewer said he was "amusing." Richard later went to Hollywood. There he changed his name to "Red."

But for Fritzi Scheff, once the toast of Broadway, there was little time left for new triumphs, only the loneliness in knowing that the spotlight had gone out and the glory road had ended.

The star for whom Victor Herbert wrote the immortal "Kiss Me Again," was still a headliner when she appeared here in 1937 in *The Prince of Pilsen.*

But thirteen years later, time had run out and the fans had forgotten. So, with her trouper's heart, she tried for a comeback at that performer's holy-of-holies, the Palace.

"There she was," reported the Associated Press, "a little old woman with a cracked voice, all alone on the stage. . . . When it was over the Palace rocked with applause. Who knows whether it was for the star she used to be or the gallant trouper she was last night?

"Who cares?"

Even as Fritzi Scheff, other names began to fade as new generations became Muny fans. But in their heyday they were part of the St. Louis story—Guy Robertson, Leonard Ceeley, Margaret Carlisle, Jack Sheehan, Gladys Baxter, Edwin Steffe, Edward Roecker.

For them, the Muny wasn't so much a stopover on the road as a summer home. St. Louis was a city to be remembered, and St. Louisans were friends as well as fans.

Irene Dunne was here for only one season but that was long enough to turn her into a Cardinal fan. She wrote that fall that she was the "chief Cardinal rooter" at Yankee Stadium when the Redbirds won their first World Series from New York.

Allan Jones was so popular here that a St. Louis businessman helped him buy up his contract from the Shuberts so he would be free to launch his movie career.

Edward Roecker, the legendary "Red Shadow" of *The Desert Song,* had his St. Louis fan club. Cary Grant and Jack Goode were familiar figures in the neighborhood around Union and Delmar where they shared an apartment for the season.

Guy Robertson returned from naval service to join the staff of a St. Louis radio station. Leonard Ceeley and Mar-

Guy Robertson was a leading baritone in 1932.

Irene Dunne was one of many stars who appeared at the Muny, shown here in 1926.

garet Carlisle were married after co-starring here in the 1930 season.

Ceeley, later divorced from the popular blonde star, kept in touch with the city and once wrote to a columnist that St. Louisans "have hailed me on the streets of New York, on trains, shipboard and the American Express in London.

"It's over twenty years," he wrote, "since my Muny Opera experiences. 'American audiences soon forget'. Oh, yeah?

"Not my old (adopted) hometowners."

For St. Louis and many a star who has shone at the Muny, it's a mutual love affair.

A young Richard (Red) Skelton was a hit at the Opera.

Mary Wickes played Katie in *Meet Me in St. Louis*, 1977.

Gretchen Wyler, shown here in 1966, has been popular with Muny audiences.

Bob Hope returned to the Muny in 1958 to appear in *Roberta*, the show that had started him on the road to fame.

ECTOR

The Grand Ole Opry, starring Roy Clark, was one of several special shows to play at the Muny in recent years.

Bob Hope has returned on special occasions. Here he cuts up with some of the cast.

The original *Odd Couple,* Tony Randall and Jack Klugman, appearing at the Muny in 1975.

The famous duo of Rodgers and Hammerstein appear
here.

Florence Henderson sings to the Trapp children in
the 1968 production of *The Sound of Music*.

Carol Burnett and Rock Hudson were enormously popular guests in the 1974 version of *I Do! I Do!*

Marc Scott is the fiddler and Zero Mostel is the irrepressible Tevye in *Fiddler on the Roof,* the all-time Broadway hit which played at the Muny in 1976.

Zero Mostel, as Tevye the milkman in *Fiddler on the Roof,* champions the cause of tradition.

Debbie Reynolds in
Irene, 1973, abound-
ed with energy.

Debbie Reynolds re-
ceives acclaim in her
1973 version of
Irene.

Pearl Bailey was a smash hit in her straight-from-Broadway version of *Hello, Dolly!*

Pearl Bailey as Dolly, is giving a lecture to her client, portrayed by Cab Calloway in *Hello, Dolly!*

Margot Fonteyn appeared here with the Royal Ballet.

In recent years dance troupes from Eastern as well as Western nations have been enthusiastically received, and have allowed Muny fans to see such performers as Rudolph Nureyev.

Cary Grant appeared in *Nina Rosa* in 1931.

Chapter 4

This Is Show Business

WHEN the Muny was just a child, it was adopted, for a time, by fabled Shubert's Alley. During its first decade it had gained national attention as America's first civic outdoor theater, and now it was to become a bit of Broadway, the western terminus of Forty-second Street.

Down the road in those depression years of the early 1930s came actors and singers, headliners and neophytes, led by two members of the theatrical family themselves, J. J. Shubert and his nephew, Milton. For many who were unemployed during the summer, it was a chance to get more stage experience and pick up pay checks. For some, it was a giant step to stardom as the Muny became their springboard to Broadway or Hollywood.

The Shubert connection with St. Louis, while born of trouble, was destined to change the Opera's personality and direction, shape it into its present form and enhance its image. It was, in fact, a turning point, a move from repertory to star system, the beginning of the new, modern Muny.

After a stumbling start, things had been going well and by the mid-20s, the season's attendance was nearing the half-million mark. But in 1929, trouble was waiting in the wings. One actress learned from a newspaper story that she had "resigned," so she left in a huff. Two others walked out, one claiming her roles were not "suitable." The stage director and the musical director were feuding. Productions weren't up to standard and ticket sales were off.

And so, in 1930, the Association reorganized the Muny and brought in Milton J. Shubert as productions director with authority over both stage and musical directors. The late Paul Beisman was named business manager, thus beginning his own legendary career with the Muny.

Scarcely out of his teens, but already a showman, Shubert told St. Louis that the Muny presented "a challenge to the creative artist in the theater, the likes of which does not exist in all America."

When he got off the train at Union Station, he predicted that "the matured plans for Muny Opera's season should make St. Louis the operatic capital of the world this summer."

To quiet the fears of some that St. Louis' homegrown theater might somehow become the stepchild or country cousin of sleek, sophisticated Broadway, the Association issued a statement that "the Shubert Theater Corporation will have no connection with Municipal Opera" and that "the Forest Park productions will be under the complete management of the Board of Directors of the local organization."

However, it added that "the engagement of Shubert as productions manager will bring numerous advantages and will permit drawing upon the Shuberts for costumes, properties, operas, directors and principals."

Many of the stars of that era—Cary Grant, Guy Robertson, Leonard Ceeley, Margaret Carlisle, Allan Jones and other local favorites—were under contract to the Shuberts and assigned to the local company by Milton and, later, his uncle who came in 1931 as productions director and remained several seasons.

The cross-country tie between Shubert's Alley and Forest Park was fashioned by three of the Muny's founders who still were active members of the Board: Arthur Siegel, Max Koenigsberg and M. E. Holderness.

Milton Shubert, nephew of J. J. who was an innovator with the Muny, brought the romantic musicals with singable songs to St. Louis, and had the revolving stage constructed.

During the 1930s, the Muny had a "New York connection" through J. J. Shubert, who made it possible for some new talent to move from the Muny to Broadway.

53

Here work moves forward on the largest revolving stage in the world.

Madame Pompadour in all its continental style was presented in 1930 and 1945.

Marvin E. Holderness was one of the Board of Directors' members for the Muny who helped give direction to its productions.

Milton Shubert, said Siegel, was "acquainted with the ability and special qualifications of all leading artists.

"We want the local productions," he continued, "to be properly cast even if we have to bring in an entirely new group of principals each week."

The Shubert system was a semi-stock company, with occasional stars imported from the East and others, here for the summer, assigned different roles each week.

With typical Shubert flair, Milton sent an advance retinue of assistants, including his own musical and stage directors and his costume designer, Orry-Kelly, later to design for film stars in Hollywood's gilded era.

It was a typical Shubert season, full of romance, singable love songs, extravagant costuming and scenery and pleasantly pallid plots.

"New York has done nothing so ambitious as St. Louis will do this season," Milton had predicted. "Even Salzburg, where Max Reinhardt has achieved the ultimate in European productions, will not offer anything more completely in the modern manner than the operettas we shall stage in Forest Park."

All of his flamboyant forecasts may not have come true, but there is no doubt that it was a successful season. A record number of 650,000 saw the ten shows which began with *Nina Rosa*, ended with *Show Boat*, and included the American premiere of Frederick Lonsdale's translation of the original version of *Madame Pompadour*, by Leo Fail.

In a *New York Times* article that summer, Shubert was credited with using " 'Times Square' methods to rejuvenate St. Louis' alfresco entertainment in Forest Park.

"It is interesting to note," the *Times* reporter wrote, "what were the changes inaugurated by Mr. Shubert which successfully brought the opera over from the non-professional red into the professional black—in other words, net profits. For there is no doubt that the St. Louis Municipal Opera is this season on a paying basis. Its 9,500 seats are filled almost every night and frequently there are a thousand or more standees. . . .

"He ordered the installation of a revolving stage (it is, incidentally, the largest in the world). This cuts the waits between scenes down from something like twenty minutes to one minute. . . .

"He discovered the orchestra was always mysteriously half a beat behind the singers, and corrected it with a sounding board which would make the orchestra's music bounce into the microphone instead of into the audience. . . .

"Then he split the stock company system. In summer many a capable actor and singer is drifting toward the coast and is eager to pick up a week or two of work at a moderate salary. Mr. Shubert took full advantage of this condition and provided an ever-changing constellation of principals from week to week."

But while he imported stars—W. C. Fields played Cap'n Andy in *Show Boat* for a $4,000 weekly paycheck—many of the performers were appearing week after week, playing one role each evening and rehearsing another each day.

Shubert, who died in 1967 at the age of sixty-six, always said that the 1930 Muny season was one of his "greatest theatrical successes." Years after the relationship between the Shuberts and the Muny had ended and Milton was director of public relations for the family business, he put up a sign in Shubert's Alley in New York advertising the St. Louis opera.

"I felt it would be appropriate," he told a reporter, "if St. Louis, the crossroads of the summer theater, could be represented at Shubert's Alley, the crossroads of the winter theater."

As he spoke, he must have been thinking back to that summer when the Muny, hardly more than an infant, was brushed with the magic of big time show business and started down a brand new road.

The next summer, J. J. Shubert was productions director. He also imported stars and staff and, also like Milton, envisioned the great potential of the Muny which, he said, "offers hope for the development of a true national theater."

"Because it is fundamentally a project of the community," he told the Board of Directors, "it is a direct expression of the people's artistic desires and ambitions. Because it is of the people, it automatically makes high standards of performance available to all."

Gladys Baxter and Archie Leach (better known as Cary Grant) appeared together in the Opera's earlier days.

Allan Jones, shown here as he appeared in 1932, remained a strong favorite at the Muny.

Guy Robertson and Leonard Ceeley star in a version of *Rio Rita.*

The Shubert hallmark, which became Broadway's imprimatur on a Muny tradition already thriving, was of exuberance, extravagance and, often, experimentation. A Shubert show's melodies were the love songs of Vienna and the jaunty toasts of debonair choristers in a beer garden. It was all lovely escapism for a summer night, a brief period spent in the world which suffered only enough trouble to make a good plot, where romance was king, the hero won the heroine, and what problems they had could be swept away on the wings of a serenade.

J. J. Shubert, the consummate showman, gave St. Louisans such favorites as the Ziegfeld hit, *Rio Rita,* but with a lavish hand seldom seen, up to that time, west of the Hudson. The reigning New York prima donna, Ruth Altman, was imported as the star, and the eye-popping sets included a whole cabaret floating on the Rio Grande.

For *The Circus Princess,* he hired a professional performing troupe to turn the Muny stage into a garish big top so authentic that spectators could almost taste the peanuts.

But Shubert was too astute in the merchandising of make-believe to rest on yesterday's laurels, no matter how successful. He also was peering beyond the horizons, gambling on public acceptance of something different. He seasoned the delicious fare of the familiar with the zesty flavoring of the new and untried.

In his second season, 1932, he pulled out of the file drawer a musical his corporation had commissioned earlier, waiting for a more propitious economic climate before going into production. The play was destined to become a Muny favorite.

It was *Cyrano de Bergerac.*

Shubert's world premiere on the Muny stage of the Samuel D. Pokrass-Charles O. Locke adaptation of the Edmond Rostand classic was "a smashing hit," wrote one critic. The singing of young Allan Jones as Christian was "of the highest order," wrote another.

The next year he presented two world premieres, an original, *Beau Brummell,* which starred Leonard Ceeley, and a musical version of the play in which Joseph Jefferson became a Broadway legend, *Rip van Winkle,* with Joseph Macaulay in the title role.

Scenic designer Watson Barratt tripled the acting area of the stage (already the world's largest) to accommodate the papier-maché peaks and rocks and winding trails in "Rip's" Catskills.

The Shuberts' innovative pattern would be expanded, refined and, sometimes, reversed by those who followed them: Laurence Schwab, Richard Berger, John Kennedy, Glenn Jordan, and the present productions director, Edward M. Greenberg.

Each, over the years, would add his unique stamp and greatly influence the Muny's direction.

Schwab, one of the outstanding playwrights and producers of the 1920s and 1930s, became productions director of the Muny in 1935. He changed the semi-stock company policy of the Shuberts, adopted a star system, and promised to turn St. Louis into "the summer Broadway of the nation."

At the beginning of his first season here, Ward Morehouse, drama critic of the *New York Sun,* visited the Muny, termed it a "compelling spectacle," and wished that "Ziegfeld could have seen this."

"There's an open air theater in this town," Morehouse wrote. "It's built on a natural hillside and is encircled by poplars and beautiful pagodas. It's in the center of a park six miles or so from the west bank of the great Mississippi. . . .

"That's the picture—10,000 persons in a great concrete bowl, a summer night, a pale Missouri moon, a musical show being performed upon a gigantic revolving stage. . . .

"Whatever the stage production, whether it be light opera, grand opera, Shakespeare, or one of Laurence Schwab's zestful musical comedies, the audience itself is the show."

Among the principals Schwab brought to the Muny were Evelyn Herbert, Gladys Baxter, Audrey Christie, Gertrude Niesen and Jack Whiting.

Two world premieres, presented in the company of some of the most distinguished guests in Muny history, were highlights of the tenure of Richard Berger, former assistant to Schwab, who succeeded him in 1936 and remained until he went to Hollywood as a producer just before the beginning of World War II.

When Berger staged Jerome Kern's *Gentlemen Unafraid* to launch the 1938 season, Secretary of War Harry H. Woodring, U.S. Senator Bennett C. Clark of Missouri, and Governor Lloyd C. Stark were in the audience. While Kern himself could not attend because of illness, the show's librettists, Oscar Hammerstein and Oscar Harbach, were here for the opening performance and were introduced from the stage.

Laurence Schwab himself came back in June, 1941, to see the world premiere of Sigmund Romberg's ill-fated musical, *New Orleans*. Romberg and Hammerstein, who wrote the book, also were here for what they hoped would be the customary out-of-town tryout before going on to Broadway.

John Shubert, J. J.'s son, and Georgette Cohan, George M.'s daughter, also were in the Broadway contingent. Max Gordon termed it "the most finished first-night performance" he had ever seen and announced he would plan to produce it in New York that fall.

He kept his word. But by the time it opened in Manhattan, the book had been rewritten, the period of the plot had been changed and it had been re-christened *Sunny River*.

It turned out to be an inappropriate title for that time in history. *Sunny River* opened December 4, 1941. It closed after thirty-six performances. America had gone to war.

The longest tenure of any productions director of the Muny's past was served by John Kennedy—one year over a quarter of a century.

In his book, *Curtain Time in Forest Park*, M. E. Holderness wrote of Kennedy's work:

"If Mr. Kennedy . . . were asked to mention outstanding productions, he probably would choose *Carmen, The Mikado* and *The King and I*. *Carmen* because he believes it represents the Municipal Opera as no other work does . . . *The Mikado* because in the presentation of this operetta he successfully overcame all the difficulties of staging an intimate book and score in the vast amphitheater . . . *The King and I* because he was able to reproduce it with comparatively no artistic difference from that of the New York production, one of the great modern plays with music."

When Glenn Jordan, general director of the St. Paul Civic Opera, came to the Muny following the 1967 season to succeed Kennedy—who had resigned to open his own theatrical production and advisory service—he adopted the policy of engaging several musical and stage directors and choreographers for the season, each to participate in only a portion of the shows.

His own appointment coincided with a time of change in the theater.

"All theaters are changing around the country," he said. "For one thing, the Broadway theater is not creating enough product. We've got to find answers for summer theater outside Broadway."

Jordan's first season here was marked by a blend of the old and the new, the traditional and innovative. *The Merry Widow* came back to the Muny that year. So did *Show Boat,* starring Arthur Godfrey. But, in a radical departure, Herb Alpert and the Tijuana Brass were here for a special one-night show at midseason.

Through the tenure of Edward M. Greenberg, executive producer, the change has continued as the Muny keeps in step with the new directions of the American musical theater. Through the years, it has moved from comic opera to musical comedy, through the period of production of its own shows— when hundreds of dancers and singers would try out for the huge choruses—to pre-Broadway engagements, dance attractions, individual starring attractions and entire Broadway shows lifted from New York for a week and set down in Forest Park.

First to be brought directly from Broadway, in one of the exciting innovations of the American musical, was *Hello, Dolly!* starring Pearl Bailey and Cab Calloway. Others which were closed temporarily in New York and presented at the Muny were *Promises, Promises, Applause, Follies, Seesaw, Irene, Over Here,* and *Chicago.*

St. Louis became the "New Haven" of the Midwest, the tryout city, for these shows which went on to New York: *Lorelei, Gigi,* a new version of *Good News, Mack and Mabel* and *The Baker's Wife.*

The bright and brittle tones of the Tijuana Brass in 1968 heralded another Muny innovation, a series of individual or group performances in contrast to the acting and singing troupes in light opera or Broadway musicals. Among those who have appeared on stage as stars of their own shows are Liza Minnelli, Mitzi Gaynor, Carroll O'Connor, Burt Bacharach, Dinah Shore, Carol Burnett and Sonny and Cher.

Leonard Bernstein, director of the New York Philharmonic, makes a dramatic appearance.

For the first time, in 1976, it brought to Forest Park distinguished conductors Leonard Bernstein and Andre Kostelanetz, directing the New York Philharmonic. In rollicking contrast was the "Grand Ole Muny Opry," starring Roy Clark, Mel Tillis, and Minnie Pearl.

In 1967, the Muny introduced the tradition of adding an outstanding dance company to the summer season, beginning with Dame Margot Fonteyn and Rudolph Nureyev and The Royal Ballet, and continuing with The Moiseyev Dancers, The Stuttgart Ballet, Ukrainian Dance Company, The Bolshoi Ballet, The Russian Festival of Music and Dance, and The Dutch National Ballet.

Over the years, beginning in 1934 with an original musical, *The Beggar Princess,* by St. Louisans Noel Poepping and Sylvester Maguire, the Muny has presented fifteen world premieres, eight American premieres and five world stage premieres of film musicals.

From stock company to the star system, from *Bittersweet* to Broadway imports, from country music to the Philharmonic, from *Robin Hood* to The Royal Ballet—show business and the Muny have sung and danced a long, long way together.

64

Paul McGuire is at work in the scenic studio at the Muny.

Scene designer Paul McGuire examines his set for *Meet Me in St. Louis*, a show produced twice in the city of its setting.

Last minute touch-ups sometimes are necessary even during a dress rehearsal.

The singing ensemble rehearses the songs for a new show.

An orchestra rehearsal is held on the platform, conducted by Edwin McArthur.

This is the inside look at the ladies' ensemble dressing room.

Here is the electric control board room at stage left at the Muny.

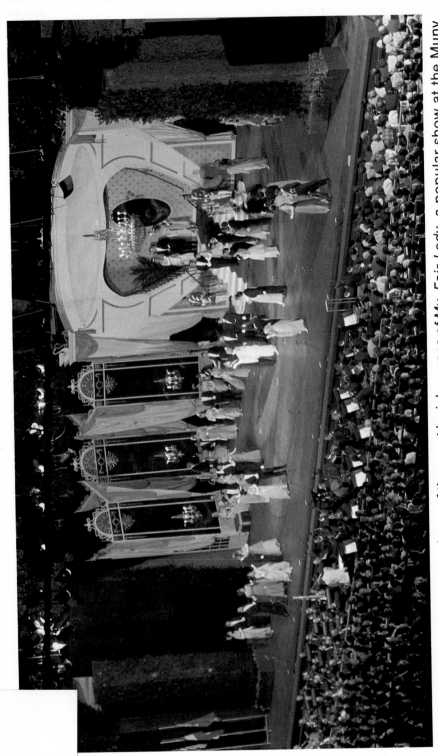

This is the grand entrance and one of the most lavish scenes of *My Fair Lady*, a popular show at the Muny.

Eddie Albert and Margot Moser have an encounter in *My Fair Lady*, a well-received show.

Margot Moser in *My Fair Lady* sings of a better life in "Wouldn't It Be Loverly?"

Society ladies float by in *Gigi*, a popular 1973 production.

Enthusiastically received by St. Louis audiences was David Merrick's *Hello, Dolly!* starring Cab Calloway and Pearl Bailey.

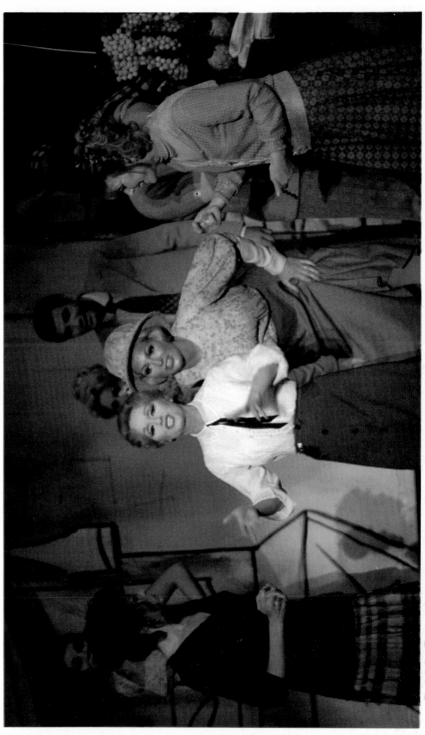

Debbie Reynolds appears in this version of *Irene*, a show that has played six times at the Muny.

Gene Kelly, a popular Muny star, appeared in this production of *Take Me Along*.

Lauren Bacall appears in *Applause* in 1971.

This dialogue takes place in *Promises, Promises*, a 1970 hit.

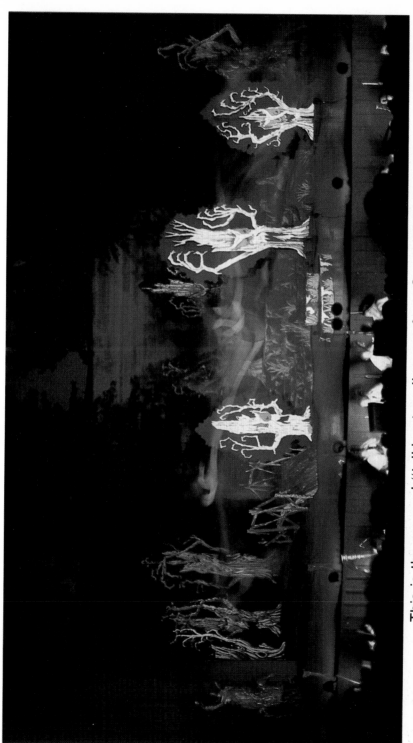

This is the unusual "talking trees" scene from *Snow White and the Seven Dwarfs*, produced twice in St. Louis, 1969 and 1972.

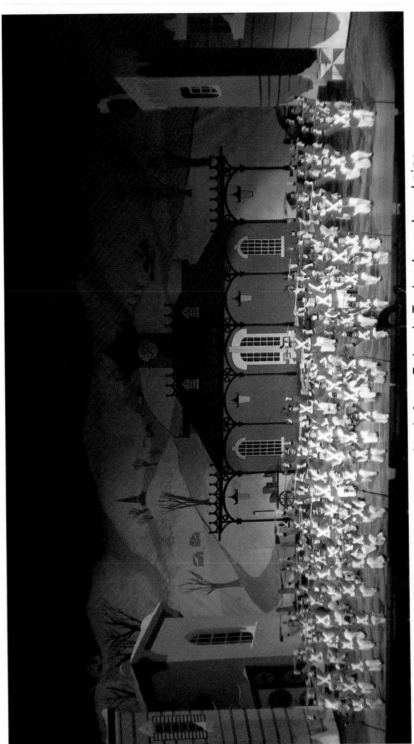

This spectacular number is from *Babes in Toyland*, produced nine times at the Muny between 1920 and 1963.

Twice the patriotic 1776 played in St. Louis, once during the Bicentennial year. Featured here are Howard DaSilva as Benjamin Franklin and Peter Graves as John Adams.

Porgy and Bess received high praise for its quality.

Players are all dressed up in *Porgy and Bess.*

Judith McCauley adds a lively touch to *Show Boat*.

Arthur Godfrey, the man in blue, appears in *Show Boat*, one of ten productions of this show at the Muny.

The bright and lively dancing chorus enhances *Can-Can*.

Lovely Dolores Gray appeared here in a version of *Can-Can*.

Here is Zero Mostel who helped make *Fiddler on the Roof* a classic.

Six times the popular *King and I* played before enthusiastic audiences, here featuring Yul Brynner who has made the part famous.

Ethel Merman is "sworn in" as President in *Call Me Madame*, a show brought to St. Louis three times, 1954, 1958 and 1968.

Walter Cassel appears here in *Countess Maritza*, performed in 1952.

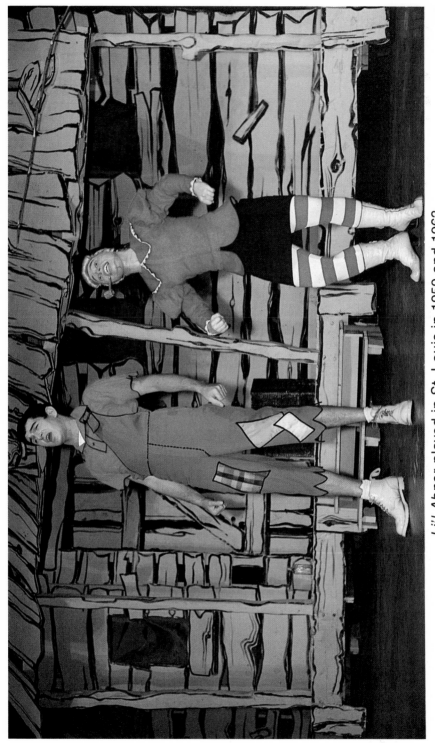

Li'l Abner played in St. Louis in 1959 and 1963.

The Student Prince, another top show with St. Louisans, played nine times over the years.

Another popular show, *Rio Rita*, found its way to the Muny seven times.

Chapter 5

Castles in the Air

THE Muny is a mime with a thousand faces, a gifted actor with an ever-changing countenance.

To the viewers in those nearly 12,000 seats in the amphitheater, the stage can turn into the Palace of Versailles or a basement apartment in Manhattan. It can be a full-sized Natchez mansion, an ocean-going battleship or a trolley. It can revolve in ninety seconds from a sheikdom to the seashore or from a beach to a ballroom.

Over the years, its scenic designers and crew, whose artistry blends the honesty of a hammer with the illusion of a shell game, have moved mountains, built castles in the air, and opened windows on the world.

They created a full-sized swimming pool for one show, an orchard of apple trees in bloom for another. A showboat, when turned around, suddenly became the interior of a theater and a steamboat was designed so, as a part of the action, it could be taken apart, piece by piece, at every performance.

The Muny's backstage miracle makers have simulated twenty-foot high Tyrolean Alps, a twenty-five-foot Oklahoma

Technological advances through the years allowed for a balloon ascension in the 1962 production of *Around the World in Eighty Days.*

silo, police and fire stations and night club facades and interiors, ice cream stores and castles. They build the equivalent of several ordinary houses every week and use enough paint in a season—3,500 gallons—to apply traffic stripes to 200 miles of concrete.

Furniture, accessories, and backdrops must be super-sized or, on the massive stage, they'll look like peanuts from the higher rows. The sets are so tall that painters work from a four-story iron dock.

The mechanical marvels are just as impressive. For *Around the World in Eighty Days,* a balloon carrying two men ascended high over the stage, with the help of a crane. A real helicopter hovered over *Superman.*

In its sixty years, the Muny's stage production technology has progressed from flimsy flats carried laboriously while the audience waited restlessly for the scene to be changed, to the efficiency of a factory producing giant scenic effects and intricate, ingenious mechanisms on an around-the-clock schedule during the opera season.

The usable portion of the stage is 110 feet wide and ninety feet deep and, literally, as high as the sky itself. Once they built a portable arched bridge across the stage, strong enough to hold thirty men.

In the center of the stationary platform is a revolving stage, built some thirty years ago. Largest such stage in the world, it's forty-eight feet in diameter and can make a complete turn in ninety seconds, permitting almost instantaneous scene changes.

Two sets of sliding booms, operated by the touch of a button, move from the wings to the center of the stage to give the designer greater flexibility in creating scenic effects.

When the Muny began sixty years ago, shows were lasting past midnight because the awkward flats had to be carried by hand and put in place. Today, sets can be built on each side of the revolving stage so that a half-turn transports the audience immediately into another make-believe world.

Watson Barratt, the late designer who was with the Muny from 1932 to 1934 and from 1941 to 1951, was credited with being the first to capitalize on the scenic potential of the great outdoor stage. Barratt, for *Rip van Winkle,* built a mountain of chicken wire for Rip to climb. Then, as the stage moved in its orbit, Rip was seen coming down on the other side.

"The audience can't be transported to the other side," Barratt explained, "so we bring the other side of the mountain to the audience."

Many sets are constructed on trucks which move on rubberized casters and are weighted and balanced delicately so they can't be blown over by a wayward wind in the middle of an aria. Painted surfaces are waterproofed with acrylic paint.

While the designer may dream up the scene in his imagination, he must translate that dream into precise measurements on blueprints, to be translated, in turn, into boats and orchards and store fronts and ballrooms. For intricate mechanisms, scale models must be made in advance so the director can be sure they will function properly.

Each of the men who has held the responsibility of creating scenic illusion since the Muny began to create its awesome and delicately-engineered sets—Barratt, Paul McGuire, Lawrence Reehling and the present production design head, Grady Larkins—has faced the unique problems of size and time and has learned to telescope both.

In one show, Barratt said in an interview, three sets were built on the revolving stage and as the lights were dimmed at the end of each scene, the stage would revolve just enough to bring a new view to the footlights. Then, as each set was wheeled out of sight, it would be dismantled and another put on in its place while the show was continuing on the other side of the circular stage.

McGuire, like Barratt before him, and Reehling and Larkins afterward, was torn between admiration for the majesty and beauty of the famed oak trees at either side of the stage and worry about how to fit them into the scene or disguise them. Otherwise, they can appear to be growing right out of the Atlantic Ocean or in the middle of a ballroom.

For Reehling, the creation of illusion on the massive Muny stage offered an extra challenge inasmuch as his design experience had been at the other end of the scale, with puppets.

But, as he told an interviewer, "the stage doesn't seem so big when you see the size of the whole theater. It's a matter of keeping everything to scale."

Technical crews at the Muny work in paint or carpenter shops or in the vast back lot bounded by the stage on one side and the administrative buildings on the other. Here you may see men working on a castle tower while nearby is the keel of a boat and on the other side of that a backdrop for a night club. Like a Hollywood lot, the working area is, in itself, a fantasy, its colorful bits and pieces of make-believe standing by for their hour on stage.

Chapter 6

Paint Your Wagon

THEY air-conditioned the outdoors at the Muny, an engineering feat which isn't surprising when you realize they built the permanent amphitheater in forty-two days, and some of those were rainy.

They also built giant pergolas and shelters to serve as umbrellas for 15,000 people in order to thwart the weatherman, who has interrupted many a performance with showers and who, at the very beginning, tried to wash the Muny right down the Mississippi.

The Opera's founders didn't envision such refinements in 1919 when they launched their civic cultural venture in the amphitheater which three years earlier had been the sylvan site of a Shakespearean comedy and in 1917 had been transformed into a permanent structure for Verdi's opera, *Aida*. Under direction of Park and Recreation Commissioner Nelson Cunliff, concrete for the permanent seating tiers had been poured in little more than a month, despite occasional showers which interrupted the work.

Twenty years later, when major improvements were dedicated, Mayor Henry Kiel was to look back and recall that "we never dreamed, nor could a seer have envisioned the miracle, that our opera would grow to such a shining success to warrant the erection of this magnificent edifice to house it."

The original structure was almost primitive in its simplicity, but from the very beginning there has been an almost continuous building and improvement program.

Today, it is one of the world's outstanding outdoor theaters, its natural beauty and spoon-shaped symmetry enhanced by technology. Yesterday's rustic hillside and grassy sward have become a sophisticated enterprise of world renown, a spacious theatrical city which each summer is alive with the sound of music.

With thousands of buckets of paint, hundreds of blueprints and scores of engineering and mechanical miracles, the Muny's staff has maintained the theater's beauty and utility, expanded and improved its facilities throughout the six decades of its existence.

But in addition to the day-to-day, year-to-year maintenance program, major rehabilitation projects have kept the Muny in the vanguard of the world's great cultural and entertainment entities.

It is the world's first (and, probably, only) air-conditioned outdoor theater. Huge fans, turned on at intermission, pull fresh, dry air from the upper atmosphere to replace moist air nearer the ground in order to reduce humidity.

Large blowers were installed to draw fresh air from outside and circulate it into the lower areas of the amphitheater. These blowers, so quiet they can be kept on during the performance, circulate 100,000 cubic feet of air a minute.

Improvements to the property began before the Opera was a year old. In the spring of 1920, Doric columns were built across the back of the amphitheater. In 1921, a new stage was constructed on concrete piers and two years later, the first amplification system was installed.

When the Muny was ten years old, the city began to worry about its condition. The *St. Louis Globe-Democrat* editorialized: "A period of permanent buildings must be looked forward to; equipment that will stand the wear of years; decorative features that will grow more beautiful with age

Super fans were installed in 1957 to help cool the air of the theater.

and will provide enlargements that are bound to come."

But it was not until the mid-30s, when the worst of the depression was over, that light towers on either side of the stage were replaced by forty-five-foot steel and stucco pylons, with space for electrical and amplifying systems.

In 1939, the Muny put on the lovely face which it retains to this day. It was created by architects Joseph D. Murphy and Kenneth E. Wischmeyer, winners of a competition sponsored by the Municipal Theatre Association, and the modernized structure was dedicated in an impressive ceremony on May 28.

This was the rehabilitation program which provided pergola shelters to which patrons retreat when showers threaten to interrupt a show. The front was widened seventy feet, and the box office set back into a semicircle.

At the dedication, where the list of dignitaries was headed by Governor and Mrs. Lloyd C. Stark, Bernard F. Dickmann, then mayor of St. Louis, commented:

"It speaks well for the stability of our citizenship as lovers of the good things of life such as music, drama and opera, that through depression, crises and many other hardships which have faced the nation, the state and city, Municipal Opera has survived."

And, added Henry W. Kiel, president of the Association and Dickmann's predecessor at City Hall, "This beautiful structure, dedicated to musical art, is the cultural and artistic achievement of the people of St. Louis, both the guarantors and the opera-goers united in a bond of fellowship, inspirationally spurred on by the encouragement of a cooperative press in St. Louis."

Few at that gala gathering could have guessed what the next forty years would bring, that their experiment launched on the wings of a dream would have grown into a theatrical and technological marvel.

There are eight buildings in addition to the amphitheater, including two large rehearsal pavilions. In addition to the outdoor air-conditioning, a complete new sound system was installed in 1976. An equally complex lighting system permits an almost endless variation of visual effects.

In addition to the revolving stage, in itself a prodigious engineering feat, a second major installation was made in 1961 to accelerate scene changes. Conceived by Paul C. McGuire, former art director, and designed by Sverdrup & Parcel and Associates, Inc., the device consists of two steel towers, twenty-eight feet high, each with parallel booms which move easily, at the touch of a button, from the wings to the center of the stage.

Even though rains continue to haunt the hillside which was almost washed away sixty years ago, the troublesome River Des Peres has long ago been tamed and its waters diverted through giant underground pipes.

In 1977, the upper parking lot was resurfaced with asphalt.

In a recent major remodeling, the entire stage, including

1968 was the year of major renovation, including the digging up of concrete for a new conduit.

the sub-floor, was removed and the steel girders sandblasted and painted. A new sub-floor was installed and covered with a new hardwood layer.

Earlier, for her fiftieth birthday, she had been gifted with a face-lift. Improvements had been made to the old stage and the electrical system modernized.

An editorial in the daily press relayed the city's best wishes on the anniversary and the gift.

"It couldn't happen to a nicer girl," the editor wrote, "than St. Louis' grand lady."

Chapter 7

Gentlemen Unafraid

THEY comprise a stout-hearted and strong-backed quintet whose careers span six decades and blend backstage at the Muny in the salt-and-pepper tapestry of headaches and crises and thunderstorms and temperamental stars, of hits and full houses and full moons and black ink on the books.

They left five different worlds to get here: vaudeville, the legitimate theater, the circus, the newspaper and business, and civic leadership.

At the Muny, however, they have shared one title: general manager.

By the nature of their work, they also share the title of Jerome Kern's opera, *Gentlemen Unafraid.*

The general manager's day at the Muny is about as serene as *The Music Man's* seventy-six trombones, as quiet and orderly as a floating crap game in *Guys and Dolls,* and as predictable as a Bob Hope ad lib. If there's a headache waiting to be had, the general manager gets it.

In chronological order, the men who have held this post in the Muny's sixty years are: the late David E. Russell, 1919-

1931; the late Paul Beisman, 1931-1958; F. Beverly Kelley, 1959-1965; William Zalken, 1965-1974; Edwin R. Culver III, 1974-present.

Five different managers from five different worlds, but show business buffs, to a man.

At the time of his resignation in 1931, when J. J. Shubert became productions manager, David Russell, the press reported, "was generally credited with having nursed the open-air opera here from an idea to a success of tremendous proportions."

He had begun his theatrical career with vaudeville in Milwaukee and had managed the old Imperial Theater and the American in St. Louis before joining the Muny at its founding in 1919. It was a natural niche for the old time showman.

"St. Louis," he told a reporter, "has an inbred affection for light opera. This tradition is so much a part of St. Louis that it has survived in spite of the wave of jazz that has wrecked light opera in this country. For the war [World War I] with its emotional nervousness led us to take up jazz and fall out of the mood for the light, languid melody of Viennese opera."

Then, reaching back into his own memory, he took the reporter on a showtime tour of yesterday's St. Louis.

Uhrig's Cave . . . Second and Carondelet Summer Garden . . . the Kensington Garden at Union and what was then the Hodiamont tracks . . . the Park Opera Company. . . .

"At the Kensington Garden, an old time spectacle, *Payne's Fireworks,* for which a lake had been created, was offered, and George McManus, father of the man who draws *Bringing Up Father,* seized upon the opportunity. His most outstanding production was of *H. M. S. Pinafore,* for which he erected a real boat on the lake, probably the most realistic presentation of the Gilbert and Sullivan work in history.

"At the old Delmar Gardens, located where University City now stands, drama and high class opera were offered in opposition. On one side was drama with Nat Goodwin, Mrs. Leslie Carter, and James O'Neill packing them in. On the other side was the light opera theater with Raymond Hitchcock, De Wolf Hopper, and Grace Van Studdiford drawing the crowds. Then, as now, St. Louis was the true summer theater center of the United States."

Russell later managed the Chicago Civic Opera House and at the time of his death in 1939 was a ticket agent at Chicago's Bismarck Hotel. His second wife, the former Marion Garvey, had been a member of the Muny chorus when they married in 1929.

* * *

They called him St. Louis' "Mr. Theater," the affable, unflappable Paul Beisman, who rose from ticket seller to the ranks of America's top showmen and from a teenaged press agent to the heady company of the best-known publicists in the business.

He was the new look of the old breed, P. T. Barnum in a Brooks Brothers suit, who could operate out of his hat and his hip pocket yet needed a computer to count his contacts. A genial sophisticate, as much at home on Broadway as in the newspaper office, he had friends among the doormen and the stars, among the office boys and the publishers.

Paul Beisman's love affair with show business, which was to continue until his death in 1958, began when he was a twelve-year-old newsboy at Twelfth and Locust streets and friendly firemen slipped him into the balcony of the old Shubert Theater. In a few years, enchanted beyond redemption with the stage and screen, he became an usher, then office boy, assigned to take press releases to the newspaper offices.

At fifteen, he was writing those releases and probably was the youngest press agent in the country. He continued in school and after graduation, at sixteen, was assistant manager of the American, advancing to manager at twenty-four.

On June 16, 1919, when *Robin Hood* opened the Muny, Beisman was in the box office. Twelve years later, he was manager.

And the Muny still bears the Beisman hallmarks.

It was he who reversed the early publicity policy of encouraging patrons to support the theater as a civic duty. He encouraged them to come out and see a good show.

As manager, Beisman introduced the concept of lavish Broadway shows, with big name stars, to replace the repertory company of the Muny's first years.

"The theater," he said, "should offer entertainment and nothing else."

Nationally recognized as a top theater man of the country, he was given the American Theater Wing's prestigious Antoinette Perry Award in 1948. Yet he never forgot those boyhood hours in the old Shubert Theater in downtown St. Louis, watching the stars from his seat high in the balcony.

That's when he became a showman.

* * *

"Bev" Kelley is a low-key funnyman, a solid citizen who looks more like a college professor than the flamboyant pitchman for the big top he used to be. But he's a born press agent and he would never let the headaches of the Muny managerial desk keep the cover on his typewriter whenever he thought he could get a good press for his new love.

"Most folks," he wrote an editor friend, who promptly published it, "think 'the spirit of St. Louis' is a flying machine in which a courageous young American with backing of forward-seeing Missourians wrote a milestone chapter in the sky. I think the 'spirit of St. Louis' is a living, breathing undercurrent of flavor and excitement in a modern city that has gone steady with 'Old Man River' for a long, long time.

"Nowhere is this spirit reflected more effectively than in Forest Park where for eighty-three enchanted evenings every year the newest and best of Broadway mingles with the musical magic of the golden past. Muny is the proudest address in total show business today."

Kelley has been show-crazy since he saw *Uncle Tom's Cabin* as a boy in Delaware, Ohio. But not until he was a newspaper reporter in Indianapolis and met high wire troupes wintering there did he become a circus buff. After a brief public relations stint with Clarence Darrow, the great defense attorney, he became press agent for Ringling Brothers, Barnum & Bailey Circus. In the winters, he often took Broadway shows out on the road and was with *The Music Man* just before accepting the Muny managerial post.

He has written several books on the circus, the best-known of which is *Clown,* about his friend, Emmett Kelly. He is a former national publicity man for the March of Dimes and served as a trustee of his alma mater, Ohio Wesleyan University.

110

But no true pitchman ever forgets his craft.

Kelley took a thirty-inch elephant to a Republican national convention to get coverage for his circus. The elephant's trainer, however, turned out to be a Hindu with an English vocabulary of three words.

The result, wrote a columnist, was that Kelley himself "had to be nurse to the elephant. He checked it into a hotel, rented a special bed for it and walked it upstairs."

Kelley's biggest coup was on the other side of the political party fence when he managed to get a string of white horses and a steam calliope into the inaugural parade for Harry Truman.

"Of course," he told a reporter, "all publicity material was supposed to be covered up in the parade. The name of the circus was in big red and gold letters across the top of the calliope. They gave me a lot of bunting and party emblems to put over the circus name.

"But, you know," he added with a sheepish grin, "I don't know to this day who stole that bunting."

* * *

He's a grandfather but everyone calls him Willie.

He's part Huckleberry Finn and part the Renaissance Man of show business. He collects French Impressionist paintings and once played the violin for his supper.

His first job, as a boy of eleven, with the Lyceum Theater in his hometown, St. Joseph, Missouri, introduced him to the magic of show business. It was a love which would stay with him always.

He's a dapper dresser as comfortable as an old bedroom slipper, a curly-haired pixie with a cigar in his mouth and a put-upon look on his face. They know him well at Sardi's and Carnegie Hall and the Media Club and the hamburger place around the corner. Leonard Bernstein is his friend and so are Isaac Stern and Richard Rodgers, Artur Rubenstein and Andre Previn, and Sam, the doorman; the famous and the modest. He was a guest at a White House recital by another old friend, Vladimir Horowitz.

He's a fastidious, on-the-go entrepreneur with an extra toothbrush in his pocket and a telephone attached to his ear.

He is said to be the only man in town who can watch one game on television, listen to another on radio, carry on one conversation by telephone and two in person, all at the same time, and not miss anything.

William Zalken is an ex-newsman with a showman's heart, an astute businessman with a gambler's soul. There's a nostalgic wail in his voice when he talks about the old days and a smile on his face when he thinks about the new. He loves the familiar music that echoes around the Muny but was never afraid to suggest the new and untried. As manager of the St. Louis Symphony—his full-time post before taking the Muny managership—he talked the Board into an all-Gershwin concert, a pop concert by Andre Kostelanetz, and the Metropolitan Opera.

At the Symphony, he originated the plan for Powell Hall. At the Muny, he introduced the highly successful dance programs which brought the world's most distinguished artists to Forest Park.

William Zalken also made another significant contribution to the Muny.

He created its familiar slogan: "Alone . . . in its greatness."

* * *

When Edwin R. (Bill) Culver, III was named to succeed Zalken in 1974, he didn't need someone to show him around the place. He just took off his board member's hat and put on the hat of the manger.

Culver, member of a family which has long been a part of the business and civic leadership of the community, was Vice-President and General Manager of Universal Metal Products, a division of UMC Industries, and former board chairman of the St. Louis Public Library, a trustee of Barnes Hospital and a former director of the St. Louis Symphony.

He had been a member of the Muny's board of directors for twenty years and its president for two—1968 to 1970—when he was elected general manager, fifth in the Muny's sixty-year history. He attended Community School, John Burroughs, and Culver Military Academy, and graduated from Cornell University.

112

The general managers of the Muny lead hectic but fascinating lives. There have been five: the late David E. Russell (top left) who served 1919-1931; the late Paul Beisman (top right), 1931-1958; F. Beverly Kelley, 1959-1965; William Zalken, 1965-1974; and Edwin R. Culver III from 1974 to the present.

While it was not until he took on the work of the general manager that he became involved in the day-to-day details of show bookings and star contracts, Culver's enthusiasm for the theater goes back to the era of *The Chocolate Soldier, The Merry Widow* and *The Student Prince.*

He told a reporter at the time of his appointment:

"Obviously, my tastes have changed substantially but I think they've changed largely with the times. Were it not for nostalgia, I'd probably be bored with the theater I fell in love with originally. What I've always enjoyed, though, are creativity and imaginative direction and staging."

Culver, a major in World War II, was an aide to Field Marshal Viscount Montgomery during the Normandy Invasion.

At his desk at the Muny, he has known, even in his first three years, his share of the headaches and the crises.

As with his four predecessors, Culver knows that problems will find their way to his general manager's desk. In show business, they come with the territory.

Chapter 8

The Sound of Music

THE rains may muffle the kettledrums, temperamental animals may leap into the orchestra pit, a frightened gamecock may land on a musician's head, and absent-minded singers may skip right over an aria, but the song of the Muny goes on.

From those first strains of De Koven's overture to *Robin Hood* on an enchanted—though damp—evening in 1919, the good, sweet sounds of music have been the harbinger and the hallmark of summer in St. Louis.

The reputation of the St. Louis Municipal Opera has been a magnet over the years for luminous names of the American musical theater and on the podium have been many distinguished conductors and composers.

John McGhie was the first musical director, deserving, as one critic wrote, of invisible chevrons for successfully overcoming the sometimes horrendous problems of that first, shaky season. Max Bendix followed him in 1920, and among his successors have been Charles Previn, uncle of the composer and pianist, André Previn, Jay Blackton and, for many years, Edwin McArthur.

115

Most of the musicians over the years have been members of the St. Louis Symphony Orchestra. The music has been light and serious, *Aida* and *Annie Get Your Gun, Carmen* and *Calamity Jane,* grand opera and country, classic and contemporary.

But from behind the scenes, there have been occasional sour notes.

In the earliest days of the Muny, musicians and music-lovers, aided by the press, lined up on either side of the question: Should the new Municipal Opera be more concerned with box office or raising the musical taste of the community?

In the midst of the controversy, one critic wrote:

"The question is no longer whether the Muny Theater is to become the summer Bayreuth of America but whether it can be saved next year from becoming an open air Columbia Theater (a popular downtown movie and vaudeville house). The reference is to the lapses into musical comedy, the intrusion of jazz intermezzi between acts of *Robin Hood,* the injection of ragtime song and dance skits into *A Waltz Dream* and mutilation of *Babes in Toyland* and its conversion into a revue and vaudeville show."

"At the end of the 1921 cycle," wrote Charles V. Clifford in *St. Louis' Fabulous Municipal Theatre,* "Richard Spamer, music and drama editor of the *St. Louis Globe-Democrat,* while admitting that the opera was a financial triumph, but not an artistic one, believed that it was time to change from musical comedies to something more elevating. Charles E. Galagher, one of the leading singers in the park, thought that the programs in 'the best and most beautiful open air theater in the world' should be on the same 'high level' as those of the St. Louis Symphony.

"Others were not inclined to agree. When Dr. Sigmund Spaeth of the *New York Times* musical staff attended a performance of *Fra Diavolo* on June 14, 1921, he was very much in favor of light operas, fearing that a season primarily of heavier works would be 'inappropriate' and that 'the vast cost would jeopardize the enterprise.' "

Although a proposed week of grand opera at the end of the second season was abandoned, Max Bendix, who had conducted at the Manhattan Opera House and Metropolitan

Opera, felt the Muny could "educate the city musically," and proposed a choral training school which not only would further the musical education of the students but would serve as a kind of "farm club" for the Muny chorus.

On January 17, 1922, the dream became reality when a choral school was opened at the Jefferson Memorial, under the direction of William A. Parson. Two hundred of the 276 registrants completed the course and, of these, ninety were selected for the singing chorus.

Scholarships for additional study were awarded to outstanding students, and some went on to professional singing careers. The choral school continued through 1929 when 600 applications were received and 287 ambitious singers were accepted.

One of the musical directors, Jacob Schwartzdorf, known professionally as Jay Blackton, left St. Louis for Broadway where he conducted many hits, including *Oklahoma!, Annie Get Your Gun* and *Call Me Madam*. Blackton came back in 1968 to conduct the Muny production of *Call Me Madam* starring Ethel Merman.

Like a kaleidoscope of melody, the memories of musical highlights flash across the Muny's story.

—The 1947 visit of the illustrious Wagnerian soprano, Kirsten Flagstad who, as the guest of Mr. and Mrs. Edwin McArthur, watched two performances and later, with young, hopeful singers gathered around, gave an informal recital backstage.

—Edwin McArthur's score for a new version of *Rip van Winkle,* with libretto by Morton Da Costa, premiered July 13, 1953, and McArthur's extraordinary gifts as a pianist, as well as conductor and composer, in Gershwin and Grieg programs.

—The first broadcast from the Forest Park stage, the final performance of *Sari,* on the eve of the opening of radio station KSD, June 25, 1922.

—The visits to the Muny by many of the most distinguished composers of the past half-century.

Harry Tierney, who wrote the scores for *Irene, Rio Rita* and *Kid Boots,* among other top shows, was here for the preparation and presentation of his *Beau Brummell,* which premiered August 7, 1933.

Richard Rodgers
was in town for *State
Fair* in 1969.

Henry Sullivan attended the opening of his musical, *Auld Lang Syne,* and Rudolf Friml was here for the final showing of *The White Eagle.*

Richard Rodgers was a guest at the 1955 Rodgers and Hammerstein Musical Festival, featuring the greatest works of the gifted team. Rodgers, who directed excerpts from *Oklahoma!* later wrote that "conducting that fine orchestra was a joy!"

For sixty years, the sound of music has soared from the green hillside of Forest Park. The comfortable and old, the familiar melodies that fall easily on the ear. The exciting and the new, the contemporary music that heralds new directions in the musical theater.

But none has had a sweeter sound than the songs which were sung on a midsummer afternoon in 1943, a quarter of a century after the Muny's beginning. They were songs dedicated to an old and dear friend.

On the afternoon of July 18, 1943, a white marble plaque was unveiled before a large crowd gathered in the amphitheater. It later was installed over the entrance. The words read:

"In memory of Henry W. Kiel, 1871 to 1942, through whose vision and perseverance the Municipal Opera was created for the benefit and enjoyment of all."

Robert Shafer sang "One Alone" from *The Desert Song.* The chorus sang "Pretty as a Picture" from *Sweethearts.*

And then they sang, for Henry Kiel, "Auld Lang Syne."

The doughty mayor would have loved it.

Chapter 9

Calamity Jane

THE Muny's own life story, like those of its stars, is a blend of comedy and tragedy, with a soupçon of slapstick and a pinch of melodrama.

It has known calamity on stage and catastrophe in the wings. Poignant moments, painful to remember. Hilarious boo-boos, impossible to forget.

In an early production of *Robin Hood,* the stage was so cluttered with papier maché mountains that the prima donna got lost somewhere in the scenery and missed an entire scene with the bewildered ingenue. But the ingenue, a poised opportunist, simply sang the prima donna's aria, scheduled for that scene, and scored a personal triumph.

Years later, in *Can Can,* Dolores Gray was discovered frantically trying to get on stage. The backstage area is so vast and the sets so ingeniously engineered that she couldn't locate an opening and her cue was coming up. The art director, remembering how he had designed the set, was able to pull two pieces of scenery apart to let her slip through just in time.

The same star suffered an unexpected soaking in *The Unsinkable Molly Brown*. A large bottle, empty during rehearsal but now filled and heavy, slipped from the waiter's hand. The chagrined star's acid comments fortunately were not picked up by the mike and, in her ruined costume, she managed to rally and get on with the scene.

In *The Vagabond King,* a performer recalled many years later, a chorus boy was commandeered as the hangman, wearing a black hood over his head and shoulders. At the most important moment, just as the hero walked to the gallows to place his head in the noose, the hangman got his hood twisted, couldn't see anything, took a blind step and fell off the scaffold into the ensemble.

Jack Goode, who began as a dancing juvenile in 1931 and returned over a record-breaking span of thirty-eight years, decided to become a comedian when the audience laughed at him for falling during a dance. The uninhibited comic, who made no secret of wearing a wig, once, onstage, jerked the hairpiece off the head of fellow comedian Billy Lynn—who thereupon refused to speak to him for weeks.

Jack's young daughter, Joyce, inadvertently stole her father's big scene when, sitting in a box, she squealed: "That's my daddy but that's not his hair."

A bumblebee, apparently from a hive in the rafters in the old wooden dressing rooms, somehow got into the wig of Edwin Steffe in the 1948 production of *Venus in Silk*. The veteran character actor suddenly slapped his head, did an impromptu dance and pulled off the wig. The bee was dead and the audience convulsed.

Another insect muffled a solo by an early favorite, Gladys Baxter. She had opened her mouth wide to reach the high note of her aria—and in popped a bug. Even as she choked, Gladys kept her cool. Calmly, she turned to the gaping chorus and yelled, "Sing, you dopes, sing!"

Although he has denied the story, a Muny legend is that when Allan Jones, making his debut in *The Desert Song,* opened his mouth to sing "One Flower in My Garden," not a sound came out and the song had to be cut. In his next show, *Blossom Time,* he apparently had overcome his stage fright and sang so well he was called back for three encores.

W. C. Fields appeared as Cap'n Andy in the 1930 presentation of *Show Boat.*

Too much came out when W. C. Fields opened his mouth. As Cap'n Andy in the 1930 production of *Show Boat,* he was ordered to cut out the ribald ad libs. The comedian drew himself up and intoned, "Nobody, but nobody, can tell W. C. Fields what not to say—especially after he has said it."

Another unhappy, awkward moment occurred when Wilbur Evans, a star for many years, was so affected by his father's death that he stumbled over his lines and forgot the words which would have cleared the stage.

Absent-mindedness also has caused some embarrassing moments. Walter Cassell, baritone with the New York City Opera and formerly with the Metropolitan, who appeared several times with the Muny, was starring in *Nina Rosa* in 1951. At the Friday night performance, he remembered it was payday, but he forgot an important fight scene on stage.

121

Joe Cusanelli, his would-be opponent, was left alone, ad-libbing desperately, until comedian Buster West rushed in with a pack of cards and the two sat there, playing cards and talking like mad, until Cassell was located and rushed back on stage.

When Annamary Dickey and Donald Clarke were co-starring in *The Chocolate Soldier,* they completely forgot to sing an aria which, because it is similar to another in the show, is seldom included. Conductor Edwin McArthur could do nothing but move on into the finale, and when the other cast members heard the cue music they rushed in, most of them pulling on their clothes.

Temperamental stars, animals and, sometimes, equipment have added to the Muny's production aches and pains.

The late Paul Beisman, general manager, recalled the aging prima donna who desperately hogged the spotlight.

"One of the costumes she was to wear," Beisman said, "was a gorgeous white affair that cost a king's ransom. On opening night, she saw a minor principal garbed in a white dress, a little less ornate, perhaps, than the one draped from her own shapely shoulders.

"Knowing that the minor principal was to share several scenes with her, Miss Prima Donna demanded that the second young lady appear in raiment of color. The tiff that ensued ended with the leading lady being slapped resoundingly. Perforce, the management had to pay the lesser light two weeks' salary and remove her from the theater at once, or there would have been no performance that night."

Two fighting gamecocks, in the opening scene of *Rio Rita,* got away from their chorus boy handlers. One flew over the footlights, landed on a musician's head and crowed before leading the ushers a chase through the hilarious audience.

A stubborn donkey ruined the solemnity of the funeral procession in *Cavalleria Rusticana,* a part of the 1957 "Great Music" show. Assigned to pull a mourner's cart, the perverse performer refused Monday night to go on at all. Tuesday, once on stage and basking in the glory of the spotlight, the now entranced entertainer refused to go off.

Actors pushed and pulled, argued and threatened and cajoled, to no avail. The dramatic aria couldn't be heard over the laughter of the audience. At last, in desperation, the stage manager turned off the lights and carried the donkey off-stage.

On the second night of the 1950 production of *Whoopee,* girls were riding down a steep mountainside on horses led by men, when the animals suddenly stampeded, galloped to the footlights and threatened to leap into the laps of the terrified musicians. That was the end of that number for the run of the show. The girls refused to ride again.

Two aristocratic, muscular wolfhounds reduced a dignified scene in *Countess Maritza* to slapstick. The star, Wilma Spence, was supposed to lead the handsome animals on stage, the trio strolling with proud and graceful demeanor. But the wolfhounds had other ideas. They refused to stop to let the star play her scene, and dragged her right out the other side.

A fountain was part of the stage set for the final scene of *The Prince of Pilsen.* An old one was touched up and put in place, but when the water was turned on, the fountain began to leak all over the stage. Richard Berger, the productions director, was afraid the dancers would slip on the wet stage, but he was assured that by opening night the fountain would be in first-class condition.

It wasn't. The fountain began to leak again, and Berger ran back to tell someone to turn it off. The stagehand was so excited that he turned the tap the wrong way and water spouted twenty-five feet into the air.

Water from the skies, rather than from leaky fountains, has continued to cause headaches ever since the disastrous flood of 1919. Records show an average of approximately two rainouts per season, excluding those performances interrupted by showers or called off after at least an hour. But the near-drowning of *The Bohemian Girl* has been approached a few times, with the weatherman threatening to blow the whole thing away.

In one of the earliest performances of *The Mikado,* the wind and rain descended with such violence that the actors had to hold the flimsy flats to keep them from disappearing down the Des Peres.

The record rainfall, however, occurred on the second Friday of the 1957 season opener, *South Pacific.* In a twelve-hour period, 8.54 inches fell on St. Louis, and wide areas of the community were flooded.

The Muny was in the middle of it. The show, of course, was called off, and by 9:30 P.M. backstage had been transformed into a five-foot-deep lake.

The storm blew out a generator, dousing all the lights. The telephones wouldn't work, but somehow the Fire Department was summoned and rescued musicians who had been marooned on the second floor. Others went out through a broken window and down a ladder on the outside of the building where the water was only a foot deep.

At dawn, the water had receded, leaving a thick layer of mud. Costumes for the next show, *Plain and Fancy,* were covered with mud up to the waists and had to be rushed to the cleaners for emergency treatment.

True to the never-say-die tradition begun by Mayor Kiel, the Muny staff pitched in with shovels to clean up, and the show went on as scheduled Saturday night.

The following season, audience and cast were forced to scatter when a storm hit during a performance of *Show Boat.* The boat itself, designed for the stage rather than for the river, had been built of painted muslin over wood frames. Mysteriously, despite its fragility and the wind's force, it didn't turn over.

When the wind calmed down and the rain stopped, they found out why. Some thirty members of the audience crawled out of the show boat where they had taken refuge and had waited out the storm, snug and dry.

In the early days of the Muny, after a few disastrous thunderstorms, the Association voted to buy rain insurance from Lloyd's of London. The policy stipulated that the rain had to be measured on the roof of the Railway Exchange Building where the Weather Bureau was located.

The only trouble was that six times in one week it poured in Forest Park and not a drop fell downtown. And that was the end of the rain insurance.

Some of the Muny's calamities have been far more serious, even touched with tragedy.

Ann Miller had a mishap on stage on opening night of *Anything Goes,* August 14, 1972. The performance was cancelled and an understudy, Pat St. James, replaced Miss Miller for the remainder of the run.

This is a 1938 version of the perennial winner, *Show Boat.*

In one of the most bizarre chapters of the Muny story, the action became too painfully realistic for singer Thomas Conkey. A St. Louis favorite, Conkey was portraying the title role in *Fra Diavolo* near the end of the 1926 season.

In the final scene, trapped on a papier maché mountain by pretend enemies, Conkey steeled himself for the make-believe bullets to fly. But the bullets were too real for comfort.

For some reason, unexplained to this day, one of the guns had been loaded with birdshot. When the scene was over, Conkey had twenty-three birdshot wounds in his right leg, thigh, and side.

For nearly a minute, he later told a reporter, "he stood on the mountainside in great pain undecided whether to complete the scene or hurry backstage for medical treatment. His actor's training finally overcame his natural urge.

125

"Singing the dying notes of Fra Diavolo he rolled down the scenic mountainside in the climactic death scene."

Conkey returned to the stage the next night, walking with a slight limp, while the management took extra pains "to prevent a recurrence of the realism."

The bullets were supposed to have been blanks and "the carbineers were instructed to shoot above Conkey's head, but either the shot or the instructions went awry," wrote the reporter, "for the twenty-three birdshot pierced his leather boots, went through his clothing, and imbedded themselves in his flesh."

The next day, Conkey complained only of a headache and the pain of his wounds but later in the week, according to some reports, infection resulted in near delirium, and he was able to get through the last show only with the help of others in the cast who quietly fed him his cues.

Sunday night he collapsed.

But, like a trouper, he had finished the run.

Chapter 10

Auld Lang Syne

IN the first fifty-nine years of its life, the Muny welcomed 38,180,500 guests from the next block and from across the world.

A president of the United States was here, and so was a crippled child who couldn't afford the price of a ticket. A vice president was here, and world heroes and sports stars and endurance fliers, season box ticket holders and those who stood in line for the free seats.

From their places on the concrete hillside, once a tree-shaded, grassy rise in a city's park they saw light opera and comic opera and grand opera, listened to comedy and the classics and country music. They watched the immortals of ballet, the legends of Hollywood and the star-spangled hits which had been lifted right off Broadway to be set down in Forest Park for a special St. Louis engagement.

They were here because of a long-ago World's Fair and a Pageant and Masque, a patriotic pageant and a Shakespearean play and a grand opera—all theatrical ancestors of the Muny.

Begun on a dream and a shoestring, almost washed away before it got going, the Muny was the world's first civic-sponsored outdoor theater and the spark which ignited similar ventures across America.

Six productions were given its first summer, 1919, with a total attendance of 91,695. Through the years, that figure

127

increased to a record high of 893,103, set in 1949.

Among viewers was President Warren G. Harding who watched *The Prince of Pilsen,* on June 23, 1923. Six weeks later, Mayor Henry W. Kiel announced from the same stage that the president had died in San Francisco. The performance of *The Spring Maid* was cancelled and the stunned audience and cast left the theater.

In June, 1927, Vice President Charles G. Dawes, a musician and composer himself, was a guest at the performance of *Robin Hood.*

That same summer, the slim young man who had brought world fame to himself and luster to the city of St. Louis with his flight, alone, across the Atlantic, Charles Lindbergh, watched a performance of *The Princess Pat.* With Mrs. Lindbergh, he returned in August, 1934 to see *Show Boat.*

In 1929, the gaudy era of endurance flights, two young men, Dale Jackson and Forest O'Brine, remained aloft in their plane, the St. Louis Robin, for a little over 420 hours. The Municipal Theatre Association had promised them one dollar for each hour and so, on August 1, before the performance of *The Enchantress,* they were brought to the platform and presented a check for $421.

Rear Admiral Richard E. Byrd attended the Opera on July 12, 1930, after his expedition to the Antarctic, and Douglas (Wrong Way) Corrigan dropped in on August 28, 1938.

Sharing the theater with the greats over the years have been those who occupy the free seats and the underprivileged who are the Muny's guests. Some 30,000 tickets for reserved seats are distributed each year through more than 100 St. Louis welfare agencies.

From its small beginning, the Muny has grown into a plant valued in the millions of dollars. Nearly 1,700 firms and individuals annually underwrite its financial success each year with a guarantee fund. Only twice, in 1919 and 1930, was guarantor money needed and each time it was paid back in full. Its sixty-seven member Board of Directors—none of whom is salaried—sets all policies.

Those policies, although based on the single, unchanged goal of bringing good entertainment to St. Louis families, have been shaped by the times. Escalating production costs, competition for the customer's entertainment dollar, a growing sophistication in public taste, television's creation of in-

128

stant stars—all these challenge the Muny at the beginning of its sixtieth season.

Stars are no longer willing to spend a week in rehearsal before a second week on stage for a one-city performance. This has resulted in a unique production policy and an entertainment circuit in which St. Louis and other major cities contract with stars to produce shows for the entire network.

For example, a production that is earmarked to play more than one city might rehearse in St. Louis and travel with that entire company intact to the other engagements. In another variation, only the principals might rehearse and tour the circuit augmented by choruses from each respective theater. An unprecedented policy will emerge this year as a production premieres in St. Louis and tours no less than ten other cities. All this to fill a need for bigger names, higher quality, and greater expertise.

Just as in the Muny's earliest years when frustration and anxiety and discouragement could not be drowned out completely by the sounds of music, so has its recent history been marked by discordant change in American theater—reflecting, as it always does, the calm or chaos of American life itself.

As chairman of the repertory committee and a former president of the board, Robert Hyland helped guide the Muny through the turbulent transitional era when romantic musicals were fading and more unconventional offerings, inappropriate for a theater catering to family entertainment, were taking their place. It was during this time that whole Broadway companies were transported to the Municipal Opera stage, "names" were starred in custom-tailored productions and other innovations, in Hyland's words, helped the Muny "strike a crucial balance."

Over the years, *The Merry Widow* may have relinquished a part of the spotlight to Liza Minnelli, and *The Student Prince* may have moved over to make room for Herb Alpert and the Tijuana Brass. Forest Park may have become a bit of Forty-second and Broadway, Hollywood and Vine.

But the Muny is still right where it began on that damp, cloudy evening in 1919—the right time, they said, to start something new.

They did start something new, and the good, sweet sounds of music are still heard in the land.

Kiss Me, Kate! was beautifully staged in 1966.

George M!, the musical life story of George M. Cohan, played at the Muny in 1970, starring Joel Grey.

Epilogue

This, then, is the Muny. The Muny they said couldn't last.

Sixty years of show business. Sixty years of show-stoppers and flops, and a star's genius and a chorister's hope.

Beyond its gates there may be war and depression and human anguish. But here, on this little island of make-believe set down in the middle of a throbbing city, trouble is as thin as a sheet of paper in a playwright's typewriter and pain is only as lasting as the echoes of a song.

Season's end is signalled by the strains of "Auld Lang Syne" in the softness of the summer night. The lights go down until another springtime.

That's all.

At the Muny, there's no final curtain to fall.

Aerial view of the Muny Opera setting.

Eager fans line up to buy tickets for a special show at the Muny.

A nostalgic musical in 1963 was *I Dream of Jeanie.*

This is a street scene in the 1962 version of *Molly Darling.*

The 1923 showing of *Wang* brought an Oriental touch to the city.

A favorite show in the 20s was *Spring Maid*, playing here to the audience stretched out across the gentle slope of the Muny outdoor theater.

Bitter Sweet is a good way to describe the times when this production played at the Muny in 1936.

The Muny stage is full for the finale of *The Highwayman* in 1922.

American Way played in 1940, when patriotism was beginning to run strongly.

Another show that reflected the changing times was *Sons of Guns*, presented in 1936 and 1943. In this scene, soldiers from St. Louis' Jefferson Barracks marched on stage.

Babes in Toyland was so popular that it played nine times at the Muny, here showing in 1920.

The 1920s required large singing and dancing choruses to project the sound; this was before the days of intricate sound and lighting systems.

One of the all-time favorite Muny shows, with eleven appearances here, is *The Desert Song.*

No, No, Nanette was such a hit that it has made six St. Louis appearances.

The final scene is played in *Pajama Game*, produced in 1962.

144

The *Music Man* made a lively appearance in 1971.

Joel Grey plays his famous role in *Cabaret,* a 1971 hit.

The famous ''Trolley Song'' from *Meet Me in St. Louis* floats over the large Muny theater.

An exuberant Gene Kelly plays Sid in the 1974 production of *Take Me Along*.

Cartoon humor abounded in the 1959 version of *Li'l Abner*.

Marge Champion brightened the stage in 1965.

The cushion dance from *Romeo and Juliet,* produced in 1967 and 1969 by The Royal Ballet.

Bruce Hubbard as Jake sings, "A Woman Is a Sometime Thing," while wife Clara, played by Daisy Newman, and Sportin' Life, played by Larry Marshall, look on in the Houston Grand Opera version of *Porgy and Bess*.

A full chorus gathers on the stage for a number in *Call Me Madame.*

This is the unusual stage setting for the World's Fair scene in *Show Boat.*

Appendix

Repertory

Aida 1928
Al Hirt's Impressions of New Orleans . . 1976
Allegro 1955
Alone at Last 1930
American Way . . . . 1940 (2 weeks)
Andre Kostelanetz/N.Y. Philharmonic . . 1976
Annie . . . . 1978 (2 weeks)
Annie Get Your Gun . 1952 (2 weeks)-56-62-68
Anthony Newley 1976
Anything Goes 1940-60-72
Applause 1971
Apple Blossoms 1940-47
Around the World in 80 Days 1962
Auld Lang Syne 1948

Babes in Arms 1940
Babes in Toyland 1920-26-29-37-43-
47-52-59-63
Babette 1939
Baker's Wife 1976
Balalaika 1941-43
Bartered Bride 1937-39-52
Beau Brummell 1933
Beggar Princess 1924
Beggar Student 1921

Bells Are Ringing . . . . 1959 (2 weeks)-66
Beloved Rogue 1935
Big Show of 1936 1972
Bitter Sweet 1933-36-41-45-49-53-74
Bloomer Girl 1949-53
Blossom Time 1930-32-53-62
Blue Paradise 1932
Bohemian Girl . . . . . . \ 1919-24-29-36-44-51
Bolshoi Ballet 1973-75
Boys From Syracuse 1964
Brigadoon 1950-55-63-68
Burt Bacharach Show . . . 1970 (2 nights)-76
Bye Bye Birdie 1962-66

Cabaret 1971
Calamity Jane 1961
Call Me Madam 1954-59-68
Camelot . . . . 1965 (3 weeks) 69-75
Can-Can 1957-61-66
Carmen 1953-59
Carnival 1963
Carousel . . . . . 1950 (2 weeks) 55-64-68-75
Carpenters Show . . . . 1972 (1 night)
Carroll O'Connor Show 1973
Castles in the Air 1929
Cat and the Fiddle 1933-35-45-52
Cavalleria Rusticana 1925

151

152

153

Stars

A

Edith Adams
Anna Maria Alberghetti
Eddie Albert
Jack Albertson
Elizabeth Allen
Jonelle Allen
Marty Allen
Don Ameche
Ed Ames
Andrews Sisters

B

Lauren Bacall
Burt Bacharach
Jack Bailey
Pearl Bailey
Gene Barry
James Barton
Billy Barty
Gladys Baxter
Mimi Benzell
Milton Berle
Herschel Bernardi
Leonard Bernstein
David Birney
Sidney Blackmer
Ann Blyth
Bolshoi Ballet
Eddie Bracken
El Brendel
David Brenner
Nigel Bruce
Yul Brynner
Buffalo Bills
Carol Burnett

C

Sid Caesar

Michael Callan
Cab Calloway
Joseph Campanella
Glen Campbell
Lana Cantrell
Macdonald Carey
Len Cariou
Margaret Carlisle
The Carpenters
John Carradine
Diahann Carroll
Jack Carson
Mindy Carson
Leonard Ceeley
Marge & Gower Champion
Carol Channing
Cyd Charisse
Bobby Clark
Imogene Coca
Dorothy Collins
Ethel Barrymore Colt
Roy Clark
Hans Conried
Jackie Coogan
John Cullum
Vicki Cummings

D

Cass Daley
Jacque D'Amboise
William Daniels
Denise Darcel
James Darren
Howard Da Silva
John Davidson
Dennis Day
Yvonne DeCarlo
Sandra Deel
John Denver
Andy Devine

Billy DeWolfe
Fifi D'Orsay
Alfred Drake
Sandy Duncan
Irene Dunne
Nancy Dussault

E

Andre Eglevsky
Faye Emerson
Tom Ewell

F

Douglas Fairbanks, Jr.
Alice Faye
Jose Ferrer
W. C. Fields
Margot Fonteyn
Pete Fountain
Eddie Foy, Jr.

G

Helen Gallagher
John Gavin
Mitzi Gaynor
Peter Gennaro
Billy Gilbert
Paul Gilbert
Jack Gilford
Betty Gillette
Arthur Godfrey
Jack Goode
Gale Gordon
Leslie Gore
Robert Goulet
Betty Grable
Cary Grant
Peter Graves
Dolores Gray

154

Martyn Green
Joel Grey
Betty Ann Grove

H

Margaret Hamilton
June Havoc
Melissa Hayden
Bill Hayes
Tom Helmore
Florence Henderson
Ed Herlihy
Jerome Hines
Al Hirt
Sterling Holloway
Bob Hope
Robert Horton
Sally Ann Howes
Engelbert Humperdinck
The Hudson Brothers
Rock Hudson

I

Ink Spots

J

Anne Jeffreys
Allan Jones
Shirley Jones

K

Kurt Kasznar
Beatrice Kay
Betty Kean
Jane Kean
Howard Keel
Gene Kelly
Larry Kert
Evelyn Keyes
Lisa Kirk
Jack Klugman
Andre Kostelanetz

L

Dorothy Lamour
Julius LaRosa
Carol Lawrence
Vicki Lawrence
Angela Lansbury
Michelle Lee
Tommy Leonetti

Hal LeRoy
Art Lund
Paul Lynde

M

Mary McCarty
Darren McGavin
Donna McKechnie
Horace McMahon
Barbara McNair
Elaine Malbin
Irene Manning
Marion Marlowe
Peter Marshall
Dick Martin
Virginia Martin
Daniel Massey
Virginia Mayo
Julia Meade
Kay Medford
Ethel Merman
Robert Merrill
Marilyn Michaels
Ann Miller
Liza Minnelli
Moiseyev Dancers
Agnes Moorehead
Jane Morgan
Jaye P. Morgan
Patricia Morison
Doretta Morrow
Karen Morrow
Robert Morse
Zero Mostel
Patrice Munsel

N

Jim Nabors
Gene Nelson
Ozzie & Harriet Nelson
Peter Nero
Anthony Newley
Gertrude Niesen
Sheree North
Rudolph Nureyev
Russel Nype

O

Carroll O'Connor
Donald O'Connor
Pierre Olaf

Jerry Orbach
Bibi Osterwald

P

Peter Palmer
Lew Parker
Bert Parks
Pat Paulsen
John Payne
Bernadette Peters
Roberta Peters
Marguerite Piazza
Molly Picon
Tom Poston
Jane Powell
Harve Presnell
Robert Preston
George Price
Vincent Price
Charlie Pride
Juliet Prowse

R

John Raitt
Tommy Rall
Sally Rand
Tony Randall
Jerry Reed
Charles Nelson Reilly
Ann Reinking
Debbie Reynolds
Cyril Ritchard
Chita Rivera
Pernell Roberts
Guy Robertson
Edward Roecker
George Rose
Steve Rossi
Richard Roundtree
Robert Rounseville
Dan Rowan
Royal Ballet of London
Russian Festival
   of Music and Dance

S

Soupy Sales
Fritzi Scheff
Vivienne Segal
Jack Sheehan
James Shigeta
Dinah Shore

Penny Singleton
Red Skelton
Alexis Smith
Sonny & Cher
Edwin Steffe
Kaye Stevens
Larry Storch
Elaine Stritch
Enzo Stuarti
Stuttgart Ballet
Barry Sullivan
Brian Sullivan
Frank Sutton

T

Maria Tallchief
Norma Terris

Topol
Constance Towers
Giorgio Tozzi
Mary Travers
Arthur Treacher
Forrest Tucker

U

Leslie Uggams

V

Rudy Vallee
Bobby Van
Monique Van Vooren
Edward Villella

W

Ray Walston
Ruth Warrick
Betty White
Jack Whiting
Mary Wickes
Paul Williams
Julie Wilson
Jo Ann Worley
Bob Wright
Earl Wrightson
Gretchen Wyler
Karen Wyman

Y

Bruce Yarnell
Alan Young

World Premieres

The Beggar Princess
Cyrano de Bergerac
Rip van Winkle
Beau Brummell
Salute to Spring
Gentlemen Unafraid
Knights of Song
New Orleans
The Open Road
Auld Lang Syne
"Rodgers and Hammerstein Music Festival"
"An Evening of Great Music"
Molly Darling
I Dream of Jeanie
This Is Show Business

World Stage Premieres of Film Musicals

Meet Me in St. Louis
Calamity Jane
Around the World in Eighty Days
State Fair
Snow White and the Seven Dwarfs

Pre-Broadway Engagements

Lorelei
Gigi
Good News
Mack and Mabel
The Baker's Wife
The King and I (Revival)
Fiddler on the Roof (Revival)
Hello, Dolly! (Revival)
Seven Brides for Seven Brothers

American Premieres

Teresina
The Beloved Rogue
Glamorous Night
Wild Violets
The Lost Waltz
Victoria and Her Hussar
Balalaika
The Dancing Years

Direct-from-Broadway Engagements

Hello, Dolly!
Promises, Promises
Applause
Follies
Seesaw
Irene
Over Here!
Chicago

156

Dance Attractions

1967: The Royal Ballet
1969: The Royal Ballet
1970: Moiseyev Dance Company
1971: The Stuttgart Ballet
1972: Ukrainian Dance Company
1973: The Bolshoi Ballet

1974: Moiseyev Dance Company
1975: The Bolshoi Ballet
1976: Russian Festival of Music and Dance
1978: The Dutch National Ballet

Directors

Frank Adam
Charlton Alexander
Angus S. Alston
Eugene Angert
Richard H. Amberg
Arthur B. Baer
Howard F. Baer
J. Arthur Baer, II
Sigmund Baer
John C. Baine
T. P. Barnett
Joseph R. Barroll
G. Duncan Bauman
Ludwig Baumann
Palmer B. Baumes
William Dee Becker
William L. Behan, Jr.
Louis H. Behrens
Paul Beisman
William V. Bidwill
C. F. Blanke
Frank C. Blumeyer
Arthur E. Bostwick
Robert B. Brooks
Mrs. Edward G. Brungard
Mrs. Georgia L. Buckowitz
Louis W. Buckowitz
G. A. Buder
Paul V. Bunn
George M. Burbach
August A. Busch
August A. Busch, Jr.
August A. Busch, III
B. F. Bush
David R. Calhoun, Jr.
George H. Capps
W. Frank Carter
Vincent M. Carroll
Henry S. Caulfield
John R. Caulk, Jr.

Charles J. Cella
A. J. Cervantes
Maurice R. Chambers
Harry W. Chesley, Jr.
Wade T. Childress
Edwin M. Clark
Richmond C. Coburn
R. R. Cole
John P. Collins
Martin J. Collins
Louis Comerford
P. E. Conroy
James F. Conway
Victor E. Cooley
Robert D. Corlett
Franklin J. Cornwell
J. Russel Coulter
Willard Cox
Kenton R. Cravens
Mrs. Mona B. Crutcher
Eugene Cuendet
Edwin R. Culver, III
Nelson Cunliff
William H. Cunliff
W. C. D'Arcy
Joseph M. Darst
Russell L. Dearmont
Bernard F. Dickmann
Duncan C. Dobson
W. S. Donaldson
Charles J. Dougherty
Arthur G. Drefs
Thomas N. Dysart
H. Worthington Eddy
Louis H. Egan
A. B. Elias
Wills T. Engle
John B. Ervin
Preston Estep
A. B. Ewing

E. A. Faust
Oscar B. Fischer
Clinton H. Fisk
S. W. Fordyce
Mrs. F. B. Fouke
J. D. P. Francis
Theodore R. Gamble
David L. Gardner
Russell E. Gardner, Jr.
Clifton W. Gates
Walter Glaser
Richard A. Goodson
Benjamin Gratz
S. W. Greenland
Joseph Griesedieck
Edward T. Hall
Frank H. Hamilton
W. M. Harlan, Jr.
Harry F. Harrington
Charles F. Hatfield
Lyman T. Hay
Isaac A. Hedges
C. Gordon Heiss
Charles Heiss
W. L. Hemingway
Robert R. Hermann
Philip J. Hickey
James P. Hickok
Edward Hidden
Adolph B. Hill, Jr.
Lon O. Hocker
M. E. Holderness
W. L. Holley
Clark Hungerford
Robert Hyland
George S. Johns
Jackson Johnson
Harold T. Jolley
Edwin S. Jones
W. Boardman Jones, Jr.

157

Aloys P. Kaufmann
Albert M. Keller
Henry W. Kiel
Arthur A. Kocian
Max Koenigsberg
Frank Kriz
Louis LaCoss
Fred C. Lake, Sr.
Louis A. Lange
Donald E. Lasater
Jacob M. Lashly
John H. Lashly
Carl S. Lawton
David S. Lewis, Jr.
Otto L. Lietchen
Hugh A. Logan
John G. Lonsdale
M. P. Linn
Howard M. Love
Thomas H. Lovelace
Sidney Maestre
Elmer G. Marshutz
Otto F. Mathi
John Laurence Mauran
Morton D. May
Morton J. May
Frank M. Mayfield
Walter R. Mayne
J. W. McAfee
Frank J. McDevitt
J. Glennon McKenna
Lamar W. McLeod
W. B. McMillan
Edwin B. Meissner
Louis W. Menk
Joseph J. Mestres
C. F. G. Meyer, III
Richard A. Meyer
Arthur C. Meyers
Henry S. Miller
Joseph Gilman Miller
Victor J. Miller
W. A. Miller
Stratford Lee Morton
John J. Nangle

Paul J. Neff
A. H. Niederluecke
Albert J. O'Brien
John J. O'Toole
Robert W. Otto
Fred W. Pape
Frederic M. Peirce
W. R. Persons
H. J. Pettingill
John H. Poelker
Henry S. Priest
Arthur W. Proetz
Thomas J. Purcell
Henry H. Rand
E. Lansing Ray
E. Lansing Ray, Jr.
Oscar W. Rexford
Roland W. Richards
Elzey Roberts
George R. Robinson
Carl E. Roessler
W. E. Rolfe
Charles G. Ross
Fred F. Rowden
Frank A. Ruf
Otto E. Rugg
David E. Russell
Joseph F. Ruwitch
William Sacks
Harry L. Salisbury
Boyd F. Schenk
John Schmoll
Edward J. Schnuck
A. L. Shapleigh
Warren M. Shapleigh
John C. Shepherd
Ethan A. H. Shepley, Jr.
R. R. Shockley
Arthur Siegel
E. C. Simmons
E. C. Simmons, II
E. C. Simmons, III
George W. Simmons
William N. Sitton
George C. Smith

Tom K. Smith, Jr.
Paul H. Spelbrink
John P. Soult
Edwin J. Spiegel, Jr.
C. C. Johnson Spink
Charles H. Spoehrer
Hermann Spoehrer
Hermann F. Spoehrer
Armand C. Stalnaker
A. C. Stannard
Mark C. Steinberg
Robert E. Stevenson
Ernest W. Stix
John B. Strauch
F. A. Sudholt
L. J. Sverdrup
Charles M. Talbert
Hillsman Taylor
Harold E. Thayer
Charles Allen Thomas
Ralf Toensfeldt
Raymond R. Tucker
C. Hunt Turner
C. Larry Unland
Richard W. Upshaw
Joseph H. Vatterott
F. W. A. Vesper
Asa B. Wallace
Mahlon B. Wallace, Jr.
Walter B. Weisenburger
Kelton E. White
C. P. Whitehead
William H. Whitton
Paul J. Wielandy
Charles Wiggins
M. L. Wilkinson
Eugene F. Williams, Jr.
F. E. Williams
George W. Wilson
John L. Wilson
William J. Wilson
Miss Sarah Wolf
Parker H. Woods